INSIGHT POCKET GUIDE

Krakow

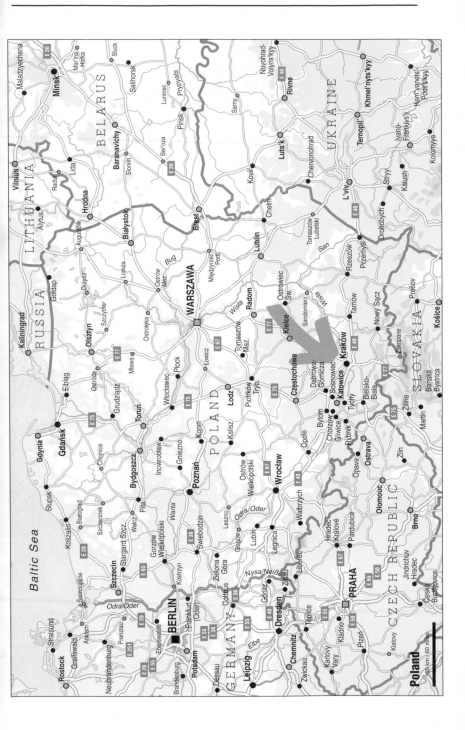

Welcome

This is one of 133 itinerary-based Pocket Guides produced by the editors of Insight Guides, whose books have set the standard for visual travel guides since 1970. With top-quality photography and authoritative recommendations, this guidebook is designed to help visitors get the most out of Krakow and its surroundings during a short stay. To this end, Ian Wisniewski, Insight's expert on Poland, has devised 15 easy-to-follow itineraries linking the essential sights and exploring some hidden gems.

The 10 city itineraries uncover the rich history that courses through the former Polish capital. Whereas the churches and museums in the city centre reflect the positive impact of Renaissance architecture and culture, the Wawel Royal Castle is a testament to Poland's frequent need to defend itself against foreign invasion. Other tours take in the influence of a once vibrant Jewish community in Kazimierz, the National Museum, the historic colleges of Jagiellonian University and the beautiful Planty Gardens. Five excursions to interesting destinations within easy reach include the holiday resort of Zakopane, the Nazi concentration-camp site of Auschwitz, a centuries-old salt mine, a beautiful castle and Tyniec's stunning Benedictine monastery.

There are, in addition, sections on history and culture, eating out, shopping, and nightlife, plus a calendar of special events. A detailed practical information section towards the end of the guide covers transport, money matters, communications, etc, and includes reviews of hotels and accommodation possibilities in all price categories.

Ian Wisniewski is a food, drink and travel writer who specialises in Poland. He is particularly attracted by the history and tradition of Kraków. 'The first time I saw the Main Market Square, the scale, the beauty of the buildings, the bustle of people and all the cafés made a lasting impression on me,' he says. In addition to the many sights, he highlights the best of the many cafés, and the most pleasant walks. And, to acquaint you with the local culture, he describes the many idiosyncratic parades and festivities that happen throughout the year. Whether you are visiting Kraków for the first time or are renewing old ties, you will find his knowledge and sensitivity to be those of a wonderful travel companion.

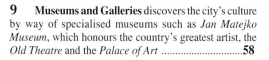

Preceding Pages: view from St Mary's Church
Following Pages: Juliusz Słowacki Theatre

History & Culture

The former capital of Poland, Kraków is still the country's cultural and intellectual centre. In the 400 years since Warsaw became the Polish capital, the two cities have become firm rivals. Krakóvians condemn Varsovians as materialistic philistines; Varsovians think of Krakóvians as pretentious snobs. Whatever the opinions in Warsaw, Kraków is both fascinating and beautiful. In 1978 it earned a UNESCO World Heritage Listing that classified 55 of its buildings and monuments as 'the highest class', and it was awarded the title 'European City of Culture' in 1992 and again in 2000. The city's 18 museums, from the Gallery of 19th-Century Polish Painting and Sculpture, to specialised galleries such as Jan Matejko House and the Pharmacy Museum, have more than two million works of art.

According to legend, a Slavic duke named Krak founded a fortified settlement on Wawel Hill, which was well-positioned on key trade routes. The earliest recorded reference is dated AD 965, when Ibrahim ibn Jakub, a merchant from Cordoba, wrote that Kraków was a major town known throughout Europe. In those days amber was a principal commodity in Kraków. It had been traded since the Neolithic era and was prized in the ancient world for its supposed medicinal benefits. It was also believed to bring the wearer good luck and both youthfulness and longevity. Salt from nearby Wieliczka (now thought to be the world's oldest working salt mine, dating from the 10th century) was another valuable asset traded from Kraków.

Tartar Invasion

Following Poland's conversion to Christianity in 966, the diocese of Kraków was founded in 1000, with the first cathedral built on Wawel Hill in the early 11th century. Wawel Hill became the royal residence in 1038, when King Kazimierz Odnowiciel (Kasimir the Restorer), the patriarch of the Piast dynasty, moved the Polish capital from Gniezno to Kraków. The Tartar invasion of 1241 dealt a blow to this fledgling capital, but it was rapidly rebuilt. The town rights it was granted in 1257 established the layout of the centre (which has remained in place), including the Main Market Square, the first buildings of the Sukiennice (Cloth Hall), a covered market and the first city walls.

Under King Kazimierz Wielki (Casimir the Great, 1333–70), the last Piast monarch, Kraków and the country prospered. It is said that Casimir found Poland built of wood and left it built of stone. Important buildings erected during his reign include Wawel Cas-

Left: Wawel Castle on the Vistula River
Right: trade flourished in the Middle Ages

tle, which was rebuilt and extended in Gothic style with walls, towers and links to the town's fortifications. Wawel Castle housed the first educational academy, established by the king in 1364, which later became the basis of the city's university. In 1335 he founded the town of Kazimierz, which became part of Kraków in 1800.

Kraków continued to thrive under the Jagiellonian dynasty (1386–1572). As Europe's trade routes became ever busier, Kraków – strategically placed at the junction between western Europe and Byzantium, and between southern Europe and the Baltic and Scandinavia – grew in stature as a capital city and commercial centre. Its significance was consolidated after it joined the Hanseatic League in 1430. Originally a commercial union of German towns on the Baltic coast, the league went on to promote maritime trade between countries around the Baltic and North seas. By the mid-15th century more than 150 towns were involved, and Kraków took advantage of lucrative trading opportunities. The resulting prosperity prompted numerous German craftsmen and merchants, including Veit Stoss (Wit Stwosz), the master carver of Nuremberg, to visit or move to the town.

The 16th century saw the development of various trades and handicrafts, and the formation of 60 guilds. Kraków's printing presses produced the first books printed in Poland at the beginning of the 16th century, and the country's first postal service was established here a few decades later. Following the marriage of King Zygmunt Stary and the Italian princess Bona Sforza in 1518, there was an influx of renowned Italian architects. The legacy of Bartolomeo Berrecci, Giovanni Maria Padua and Santi Gucci can be seen at Cloth Hall, Wawel Castle, and at various monuments, tombs and epitaphs.

An Elected Monarch

Indeed Kraków enjoys a distinct Italian Renaissance character. Its medieval defences were also extended at this time. The north of the town was protected by a barbican and linked by a double-walled thoroughfare to Florian's Gate, one of eight city gateways. The coronation of King Henryk Walezy in 1574 was a minor landmark: he became the first Polish monarch to be elected – albeit by the nobility only – thus marking the end of the country's hereditary system of government.

Meanwhile Warsaw was also rapidly developing as the capital of the Mazovian

Above: for sealing trade deals
Left: fortifications have been vital to Kraków

dukedom. More central to the Polish-Lithuanian Commonwealth (established in the 14th century) than Kraków, Warsaw was becoming a leading administrative centre. The *Sejm* (parliament) was transferred to Warsaw in 1569 and Kraków went into decline. In 1596 King Zygmunt III Waza declared Warsaw the Polish capital and transferred the royal residence to Warsaw's Royal Castle. The royal treasury remained at the Wawel, and coronations and royal funerals continued to be held in Wawel Cathedral. King August II was the last king to be crowned here, in 1734. Kraków was badly damaged by a Swedish invasion, known locally as *Potop* ('The Deluge'), in 1655–7. The royal treasury and many works of art were looted.

Partition

The opposition of various nobles to Poland's last king, Stanisław August Poniatowski, elected in 1764, heightened the country's vulnerability to its predatory neighbours. Prussia, Russia and Austro-Hungary partitioned Poland twice, in 1772 and 1793, and the country ceased to exist. Poles united and fought for independence. Tadeusz Kościuszko took a celebrated oath in Kraków's Main Market Square before leading his troops to victory over Russia at the Battle of Racławice in 1794. But a third partition, in 1795, forced the king to abdicate. The Kraków region became part of the Austrian-Habsburg Empire and Kazimierz was incorporated into Kraków in 1800.

In 1809 Kraków became part of the Duchy of Warsaw, established by Napoleon. But in 1815 Napoleon was defeated at Waterloo and the subsequent Congress of Vienna re-drew the map of Europe. Warsaw was to be the capital of a Polish 'kingdom' ruled by Russia. Kraków was given the status of a free city and capital of the Kraków Republic, which existed until 1846.

The Kraków revolution of 1846 was suppressed by the Austrians, who incorporated the city into their province of Galicia. Under the relatively liberal Austrians, Polish culture thrived, but in 1850 the Great Fire of Kraków destroyed or seriously damaged almost 200 buildings. Once again the city had to rebuild, and by the turn of the 20th century Kraków had resumed its role as the country's intellectual and spiritual centre.

In 1918, at the end of World War I, a Polish army mobilised in Kraków. Led by Marshall Józef Piłsudski, it defeated the Prussian, Russian and Austro-Hungarian forces. Poland had finally won independence. Piłsudksi acted as head of state until 1922; his state funeral was held in Kraków in 1935.

The Nazis invaded Poland on 1 September 1939. They set up a puppet government in Kraków, and the governor general, Hans Frank, took up residence in Wawel Castle. The Płaszów and Liban forced-labour camps were

Above: Stanisław Poniatowski, Poland's last king

soon established, and a number of Jagiellonian University academics were sent to Sachsenhausen concentration camp. A Jewish ghetto was established in Kraków, from which Jews were sent to Auschwitz.

Auschwitz-Birkenau comprised two adjoining concentration camps. Auschwitz was a slave-labour camp, principally for Polish and German 'political prisoners', resistance members and 'opponents' of the Nazi regime. Birkenau was an extermination camp. Up to two million prisoners, the great majority of them Jews from across Europe, together with Poles, Russians and gypsies, died here as a result of slavery, hunger, illness, torture or in the gas chambers. Corpses were burned in crematoria and buried in mass graves.

Before retreating in 1944, the Nazis began destroying evidence of their horrific crimes. They detonated the crematoria and some camp buildings, but didn't have enough time to destroy the gas chambers. The Nazis intended to raze Kraków but were foiled by a sudden advance by the Soviet Red Army. Kraków was thus one of the very few Polish cities to survive the war virtually intact. The Red Army 'liberated' the city on 18 January 1945, whereupon the Soviet troops initiated a repressive regime.

Communism

The Nazis left Warsaw utterly devastated, so for a short time Kraków was once again the country's premier city. Rigged elections resulted in a communist government, and the country became a satellite of the Soviet Union. The new regime was determined to replace the city's intellectual and cultural élitism with a new socialist spirit in the form of a vast proletarian labour force. The Lenin steelworks, now known as Sendzimir, were built in the Kraków suburb of Nowa Huta in 1947–9. The consequent pollution was detrimental to people and historic buildings alike. The post-communist regime has since introduced a tough policy of dealing with industrial waste.

Lech Walesa's Solidarity movement mounted the most serious threat to an

Above: the Nazi terror, depicted in World War II

Eastern bloc regime since the Prague Spring of 1968. Bowing to the sheer weight of its numbers and international support, the government accepted it as a legal trade union in 1980. But the following year General Jaruzelski declared martial law. This was a time of severe shortages – people had to queue all night for staples – and meat, butter and even vodka were rationed. Waiting lists for refrigerators and cars could extend for years. 'Artificial' employment provided work, however menial or unnecessary, for everyone.

Ultimately Solidarity triumphed, the Berlin Wall fell and Eastern-bloc communism collapsed. The privatisation and democracy that Poland has enjoyed since 1989 has been particularly beneficial in Kraków. Café society has returned, restaurants have boomed, shops stock top international brand names and premium-quality Polish products, and standards of service have improved. Kraków is now Poland's third-largest city, with a population of 750,000.

University City

As the 'Oxbridge' of Poland, the Jagiellonian University maintains Kraków's status as the country's centre of intellectual, youthful, bohemian life. In the summer holidays the university holds schools with courses on Polish language, culture and history for foreign students, particularly Polish émigrés. The university was established as an academy in Wawel Castle in 1364 by Kazimierz Wielki. In 1400 it became Poland's first university college. The astronomer Mikołaj Kopernik (Copernicus) studied here in 1491–95.

Kraków is a very musical city. As well as a lot of jazz and cabaret venues and clubs, there are a number of annual music festivals. The Music of Old Kraków Festival features classical concerts held in atmospheric burghers' houses, churches and palaces throughout the historic centre. The composer Zbigniew Preisner, who has written film scores for directors such as Krzysztof Kieślowski and Andrzej Wajda, served his apprenticeship at a musical and cabaret venue on Kraków's Main Market Square. The innovative Krzysztof Penderecki (born 1933) studied at Kraków, was professor of music at the Jagiellonian University and, during the late 1980s, was the artistic director of the National Philharmonia, established in 1945.

The artist Jan Matejko, who was born and spent most of his life in Kraków, was instrumental in establishing the city's Academy of Fine Arts in 1879. His pupils included Stanisław Wyspiański and Józef Mehoffer, both pioneers of the *Młoda Polska* (Young Poland) movement that emerged in Kraków in the late 19th and early 20th centuries. Kraków was also a centre for artistic movements such as the 1920s abstract group known as 'Blok'. Incorporating elements of Cubism and Constructivism, the Blok artists equated their work with communal manual labour rather than individual creativity.

In literature, Kraków has always been renowned for poets rather than novelists. The romantic poet Adam Mickiewicz (1798–1855) was not a

Right: a sartorially sound busker

Cracovian, but his monument is an important feature of the city's Main Market Square. When it was unveiled on the centenary of his birth, it was as much a statement of Polish nationalism as a tribute to one of the country's most celebrated writers. In his most enduring work, the epic *Pan Tadeusz (Mister Thadeus)*, published in 1834, Mickiewicz describes the traditional lifestyle of the Polish nobility.

The romantic poet Adam Asnyk (1838–97) lived and wrote in Kraków from the 1870s. In the 1920s Kraków hosted the Avant-Garde Cracovians poets' circle, and it's the home town of poet Wisława Szymborska (born 1923), who won the Nobel Prize for literature in 1996, while Czesław Miłosz (1911–2004), who won the award in 1980, was an honorary citizen.

Theatre and Cinema

Kraków has been the birthplace of a number of artistic achievements. A 'Mystery Play' staged in 1533 by the Dominicans is the country's earliest documented play, and Poland's first permanent theatre, Stary Teatr, opened here in the 1790s. This is now the country's oldest serving theatre as well as one of the finest. Many renowned directors (including Andrzej Wajda) have worked at the Stary Teatr, which still serves as the base of the Helena Modrzejewska Theatre Company. This troupe was founded by the legendary 19th-century actress, after whom it's named. She took Kraków, Warsaw and then the USA by storm.

The painter Wyspiański was also a playwright. His most celebrated work, *Wesele (The Wedding)*, premiered in Kraków in 1901. Wyspiański staged productions, including *Hamlet,* at Wawel Castle. Kraków's rich legacy of avant garde productions includes the celebrated Tadeusz Kantor (1915–90), a director who founded the Cricot Theatre Company in 1956. Even today, the long-running rivalry with Warsaw persists. Many Krakóvian thespians and directors won't work in Warsaw (and vice versa).

The first film shown in Poland was screened at the Juliusz Słowacki Theatre in 1896. Today Kraków's annual International Festival of Short Feature Films continues the city's cinematic heritage. The cinematic luminary Andrzej Wajda (born 1926), whose films, such as *Popioł i Diament (Ashes & Diamonds)*, *Człowiek z Marmuru (Man of Marble)*, *Człowiek Żelaza (Man of Iron)* and *Danton*, have won international acclaim, was educated in Kraków. In his early works Wajda made political as well as artistic breakthroughs. The gradual cultural thaw that followed Stalin's death in 1953 enabled the 'wartime generation' of artists and directors to allude to political issues in their work for the first time. Consequently, Wajda was a leading member of the group of filmmakers that became known for the so-called *Kino Niepokoju Moralnego* (Cinema of Moral Anxiety).

Left: students at rest

HISTORY HIGHLIGHTS

50,000 BC Early traces of Paleolithic settlement on Wawel Hill.

9th century AD Wawel Hill is established as a fortified village and the seat of the Wiślan (Vistulan) dukes.

AD 965 The earliest written reference to Kraków, by Cordoba merchant Ibrahim ibn Jakub, who describes it as a major town known throughout Europe.

AD 1000 The bishopric of Kraków is founded following Poland's conversion to Christianity in 966.

Early 11th century Construction of first cathedral on Wawel Hill.

1038 King Kazimierz Odnowiciel (Casimir the Restorer) begins to construct a royal residence on Wawel Hill, after moving the capital of Poland from Gniezno to Kraków.

1086 St Andrew's, one of Poland's earliest Romanesque churches, is founded.

12th century Wieliczka salt mine is established outside Kraków.

1241 Tartars invade and destroy the town.

1257 Kraków gains municipal rights.

1290 Construction of St Mary's Church in the Main Market Square begins.

1335 Kazimierz is founded as a separate town outside Kraków.

1386 Inauguration of the Polish-Lithuanian Commonwealth with Kraków as the capital.

1400 Collegium Maius is established as the second university college in central and eastern Europe.

1430 Kraków joins the Hanseatic League.

1477–89 The Gothic triptych altar-piece in St Mary's Church is completed.

1499 Construction of the barbican is completed.

1556–60 The Cloth Hall, designed by Giovanni Maria of Padua (Padovano) is built in Renaissance style.

1596 King Zygmunt III Waza transfers the royal residence to Warsaw, which he declares the capital of Poland.

1665–7 Swedish invaders ravage and loot the town.

1734 King August III Saski becomes the last Polish monarch to be crowned in Wawel Cathedral.

1783 Botanical Gardens established.

1795 After three successive partitions of Poland, Kraków becomes part of the Austro-Hungarian Empire.

1799 Poland's oldest serving theatre, Stary Teatr, is established.

1800 Kazimierz becomes part of Kraków.

1820s Planty Gardens are laid out after the medieval city walls are demolished.

1823 Redolfi, Kraków's oldest serving café, opens for business.

1846 Kraków leads an insurrection against the Austro-Hungarian Empire.

1850 The Great Fire devastates the town's historic centre.

1879 Poland's first national museum is established within the Cloth Hall.

1896 The Juliusz Słowacki Theatre opens and screens first film in Poland.

1905 Jama Michalika café opens, decorated in bold Secessionist style.

1918 Kraków becomes part of a newly independent Poland.

1939 Nazis establish administrative headquarters in the city. Governor general Hans Frank takes up residence in Wawel Castle.

1945 Red Army liberates Kraków. Rigged election leads to Communist, Soviet-satellite government.

1947–9 The Lenin steelworks (now known as Sendzimir) are built in the Kraków suburb of Nowa Huta.

1978 Kraków's historic centre gains UNESCO World Heritage Status.

1978 Cardinal Karol Wojtyła, Bishop of Kraków, is elected Pope John Paul II.

1980 Government recognises Solidarity as a legitimate free trade union.

1981–3 Imposition of martial law.

1989 Democratic elections.

1992 & 2000 Kraków is twice declared a European City of Culture.

2004 Poland joins the EU.

2005 The city's people take to the streets to mourn the death of the Pope.

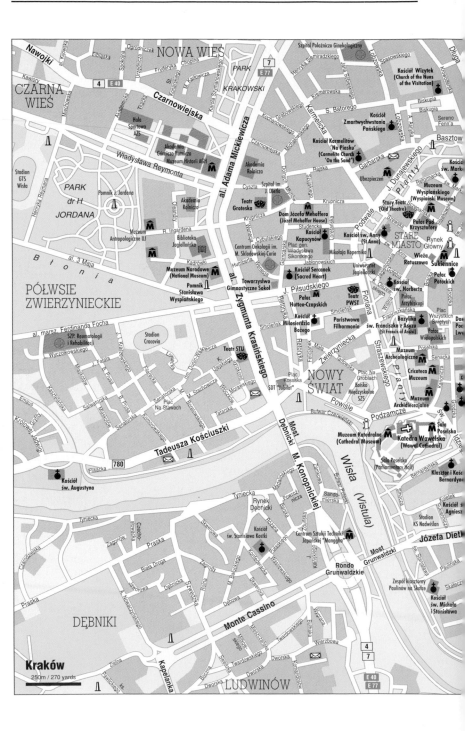

Kraków

250m / 270 yards

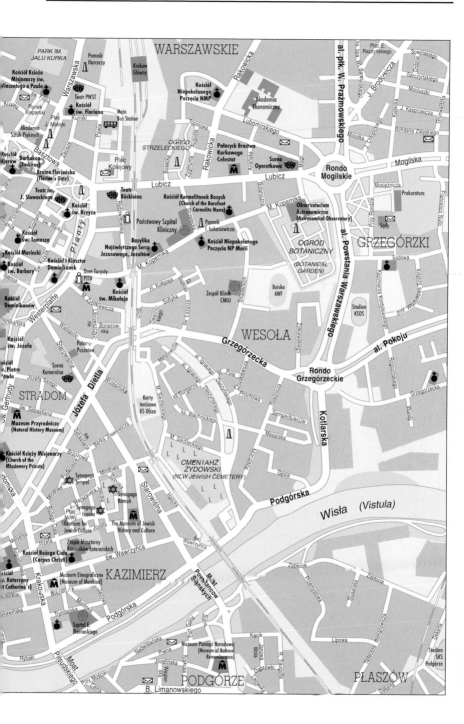

PARK IM. JALU KURKA

WARSZAWSKIE

Pomnik Harcerzy

Kraków Główny

al. płk. W. Prażmowskiego

ks. bpa W. Bandurskiego

Plac E. Raczyńskiego

Sowińskiego

J. Brodowicza

Garczyńskiego

Kościół Księża Misjonarzy św. Wincentego a Paulo

Rakowicka

Kościół Niepokalanego Poczęcia NMP

Akademia Ekonomiczna

Moniuszki

J. Kasprowicza

Warszawska

Teatr PWST

Kościół św. Floriana

Main Bus Station

Topolowa

Lubomirskiego

Bohdana Zaleskiego

Rynek Kleparski

Plac J. Matejki

Kurniki

OGRÓD STRZELECKIEGO

Pałacyk Bractwa Kurkowego Celestat

Scena Operetkowa

Mogilska

Akademia Sztuk Pięknych

Basztowa

Plac Kolejowy

Rakowicka

Mosięźnicza

Rondo Mogilskie

Kościół Barbakan (Barbican)

Lubicz

Lubicz

Prokuratura

Brama Floriańska (Florian's Gate)

Teatr im. J. Słowackiego

Teatr Bückleina

Kościół Karmelitanek Bosych (Church of the Barefoot Carmelite Nuns)

M. Kopernika

Observatorium Astronomiczne (Astronomical Observatory)

Sądy

Kościół św. Krzyża

Planty

Państwowy Szpital Kliniczny

Pomnik J. Łukasiewicza

GRZEGÓRZKI

Kościół św. Tomasza

Bazylika Najświętszego Serca Jezusowego, Jezuitów

Kościół Niepokalanego Poczęcia NP Marii

OGRÓD BOTANICZNY (BOTANICAL GARDEN)

Kościół Mariacki

Kościół św. Barbary

Kościół i Klasztor Dominikanek

Dom Turysty PTTK

M. Kopernika

Sadowa

al. Powstania Warszawskiego

Kościół Dominikanów

Kościół św. Mikołaja

H. Kołłątaja

Zespół Klinik CMUJ

Boisko AWF

Stadion KSOS

Westerplatte

Sofijki

Starowiślna

Kościół św. Józefa

Pałac Puszetów

Bonerow-ska

WESOŁA

Grzegórzecka

al. Pokoju

Kościół św. Piotra i Pawła

Scena Komeralna

Dietla

Wrzesińska

Rondo Grzegórzeckie

Grzegórzecka

STRADOM

Jozefa Sarego

Józefa

Kotlarska

św. Gertrudy

św. Sebastiana

Muzeum Przyrodnicze (Natural History Museum)

Korty tenisowe KS Olsza

Semperitowców

Masarska

Kościół Księży Misjonarzy (Church of the Missionary Priests)

Berka Joselewicza

Brzozowa

M. Siedleckiego

CMENTARZ ŻYDOWSKI (NEW JEWISH CEMETERY)

Gęsia

Synagoga Tempel

Miodowa

Synagoga Remuh

Starowiślna

Halicka

Podgórska

Plac Nowy

Synagoga Izaaka

The Museum of Jewish History and Culture

Wisła (Vistula)

Centrum for Jewish Culture

Józefa

Zespół klasztorny Kanoników Lateranskich

św. Wawrzyńca

Kościół Bożego Ciała (Corpus Christi)

KAZIMIERZ

Muzeum Etnograficzne (Museum of Mankind)

Kraków

Podgórska

Most Powstańców Śląskich

Zabłocie

Zabłocie

Kościół św. Katarzyny (St Catherine's)

Szpital E. Biernackiego

Trynitarska

Przemysłowa

Lipowa

Stadion SKS Podgórze

Piłsudskiego

Nadwiślańska

Piwna

Muzeum Pamięci Narodowej (Museum of National Remembrance)

Kącik

Jadowa Wola

Rybaki

Jozefińska

Przy Moście

Celna

B. Limanowskiego

PODGÓRZE

PŁASZÓW

City Itineraries

Kraków is remarkably compact, with the historic centre's attractions and adjacent areas of interest all within relatively easy walking distance. The centre is thoroughly pedestrianised, and even inexperienced map readers should find it easy to get around a city centre composed of a series of grid-like streets linking it to the Main Market Square. Addresses feature the name of the street followed by the number. *Ul* means 'street', *al* means 'avenue' and *plac* 'square'. Street names are usually well signposted, but street numbers can be harder to find – they're often nonexistent.

The historic centre is encircled by the Planty Gardens, a delightful stretch of greenery laid out on the grounds where the city's walls originally stood. Use the gardens as a landmark – lots of streets leading to the city centre and Main Market Square cross the Planty. The gardens are encircled by principal thoroughfares, with regular bus and tram services, though none of these actually circumscribe it. Beyond these main streets are various districts which also feature a host of historic architecture and attractions. The itineraries suggested in the following pages can all be undertaken on foot.

Avoiding the Masses

The weather is usually sunny and dry in summer and crisp in winter, although relentless rain for days at a time is also possible, so don't forget to bring waterproof footwear and clothing, and an umbrella. The majority of museums are closed on Mondays, but you should check all opening hours because they are prone to change. Many churches are open only during Mass, so if you want to avoid the crowds – thereby also ensuring that you don't disturb the worshippers – an early-morning visit is probably the best bet.

Ten suggested itineraries are designed to introduce you to the essential character and history of Kraków. These cover the historic centre and its architectural treasures, the city's numerous churches, galleries and museums, the imposing Wawel Castle and Cathedral, and the traditionally Jewish district of Kazimierz. All explore different areas and themes of Kraków, and can be taken in any order that suits your preferences.

Five excursions to the most interesting places outside the city take in the holiday resort of Zakopane, loved by skiers and intellectuals alike, the horrific site of Auschwitz, now listed as a UNESCO World Heritage site, the subterranean world of the Wieliczka salt mine, and, dating back nearly 1,000 years, the Benedictine abbey at Tyniec. These can be reached by public transport, or you might join a commercial guided tour organised by one of the city's tourism companies.

Left: the Barbican protected the city in the time of the Renaissance
Right: a traditional busker in a city renowned for its culture

1. THE HISTORIC CENTRE *(see map, p24)*

An ideal way to familiarise yourself with the city's key attractions, this round trip from the Main Market Square takes in historic streets and Florian's Gate, visiting various churches and museums along the way.

Rynek Główny (Main Market Square) has been Kraków's commercial and social centre for centuries. Measuring 200sq m (2,150sq ft), it is also one of Europe's largest medieval squares. This was once the scene of majestic royal parades, and official guests are still ceremoniously greeted here. On a more everyday level, the square is always busy with locals and tourists. In summer the buzz goes on late into the night. An abundance of cafés, restaurants, shops, flower stalls and street performers form a colourful, engaging atmosphere. On the cultured side, buskers often appear as duets and trios playing exquisite classical refrains; of a more humourous nature, don't be surprised to see beggars' placards with slogans such as, 'I'm healthy and happy, I'm just collecting money for beer.'

The imposing burghers' houses and the palaces surrounding the Main Market Square were once owned by the city's wealthiest merchants and aristocratic families. A variety of facades reflects diverse architectural genres. Poland's first post office operated during the 16th and 17th centuries from

Dom Włoski (The Italian House) at No 7. At No 9, **Dom Bonerów** (Boner House) has retained the original ornamental attic built in the 1560s, when the house belonged to the king's private banker, Jan Boner. The city's most historic restaurant, Wierzynek, at No 15, comprises two Renaissance houses. One of the dining rooms features original 14th-century Gothic arches, and the wine bar and grill is situated in a 14th-century cellar.

Above: in the Main Market Square
Left: museum in the Sukiennice (Cloth Hall)

The 16th-century **Dom Pod Obrazem** (House Under the Painting) at No 19 features a beautiful fresco of the Blessed Virgin Mary ascending into Heaven, held aloft by angels, that was completed in 1718. The **Zbaraski-Wodzicki Palace** at No 20, which houses the Goethe Institute, was built in the 14th century, though its neoclassical facade dates from the 18th century, when the arcaded courtyard was also added. Also dating from the 14th century, **Pałac Pod Baranami** (Palace Under the Rams) at No 27 was refashioned in the mid-19th century. The courtyard garden is now a popular café and the Piwnica pod Baranami (Cellar Under the Rams) a renowned cabaret and musical venue.

A fascinating collection tracing Kraków's history and culture through paintings and decorative arts can be seen in the **Museum of the City of Kraców** at Pałac Krzysztofory (Krzysztofory Palace, Rynek Główny 35; tel: 619 2300; open Wed, Fri–Sun 9am–4pm, Thur 10am–5pm, closed second Sun of the month; free on Sat). As it appears now, the palace – a suitably historic setting for the exhibits – and its arcaded courtyard date from the 17th century.

Gothic Tower

All that remains of the magnificent **Ratusz** (Town Hall) is the **Wieża Ratuszowa** (Town Hall Tower; tel: 422 9922; open daily summer 10.30am–6pm; admission fee), which also incorporates a tourist information bureau. This handsome red-brick tower is inlaid with decorative stone and is principally 14th-century Gothic, with 16th-century Renaissance additions. The main town hall was demolished in 1820, at the same time as much of the city's defensive walls and towers, and it was only due to sustained protests by prominent locals that the tower was saved. It doesn't take long to view the tower (and much of that time is spent negotiating steep, narrow stairs), and a model that demonstrates the splendour of the original town hall on the ground floor.

The first floor, originally a chapel, houses a collection of architectural fragments, though it is now mainly used as exhibition space. The second floor's photographic exhibition shows how the tower looked during the 19th century, and there are good views from here. If you're ready for a break, the former prison and torture chambers beneath the tower are now a café with Gothic barrel-vaulted ceilings, stone portals and heavy carved wooden furniture. In the summer you can dine al fresco at tables set up around the tower.

18th-century Time Capsules

At the centre of the market square is the magnificent **Sukiennice** (Cloth Hall). Originally a covered market with stalls, shops and warehouses selling cloth and textiles, this building was first constructed in the mid-13th century.

Right: Padovano's Sukiennice (Cloth Hall)

After the hall was almost destroyed by fire, Giovanni Maria of Padua (known as Padovano) designed the current Renaissance facade, including the loggias at either end, in 1556–60. The ornamental attic, decorated with mascarons for which Kraków's most distinguished burghers apparently posed, was the work of Santi Gucci of Florence. The roof also features various copper globes surmounting small spires. During recent renovations it was discovered that these globes contained historic documents from the late-18th to the mid-19th century – there is a long tradition of builders secreting items for posterity in such 'time capsules'.

The ground floor of the Sukiennice retains its commercial role. Stalls here sell folk arts and crafts, amber and silver jewellery, leather goods and superior quality souvenirs. The arcades added in 1875–9 on either side of the building now house attractive cafés. A delightful example, at No 1, is the Seccessionist-style Kawiarnia Noworolski.

The first floor of the Sukiennice houses the **Galeria Sztuki Polskiej XIX Wieku** (Gallery of 19th-Century Polish Painting and Sculpture, Rynek Główny 1–3; tel: 422 11 66; open Tues, Thur, Sat–Sun 10am–3.30pm, Wed, Fri 10am–6pm; may close for refurbishment in 2007; admission fee). Poland's first national museum, it opened in 1879. Jan Matejko, the finest painter in the country's history, was among the artists who donated their own work. This museum is quite small, but you might want to allow longer here than at first seems necessary because the collection is both comprehensive and of outstanding quality. Of the four galleries, the Sala Oświecenia (Enlightenment Room) traces the history of Classicism, the Sala Michałowska (Michałowski Room) is for Romanticism, Sala Hołdu Pruskiego (Prussian Homage Room) covers historical paintings and portraits, and Sala Czwórki (Carriage and Four Room) features landscapes, with examples of Impressionism and the Barbizon School. In addition to the works of Polish artists such as Matejko, Adam

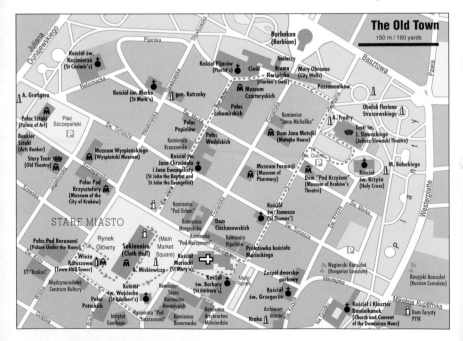

Chmielowski, J Tatarkiewicz and P Weloński, the collection includes pieces by foreign artists working in Poland, such as the Italian Marcello Bacciarelli, who was the court artist of King Stanisław August Poniatowski in the late 18th century.

Adam Mickiewicz Monument

A popular meeting point for locals in the Main Market Square is by **Pomnik Adama Mickiewicza** (Adam Mickiewicz Monument), which honours Poland's greatest romantic poet. Designed by Teodor Rygier, it was erected in 1891 on the centenary of the poet's birth. The monument is the venue for Kraków's pre-Christmas Christ Child Crib Competition which always draws large crowds. Other traditional events held in Main Market Square include the colourful *Lajkonik* pageant shortly after Corpus Christi. This sees a procession of 'Tartars' marching through the streets led by the *lajkonik*, a legendary Polish hero disguised as a Tartar riding a hobbyhorse that dances to the beat of accompanying drums. It's considered good luck to be touched by the *lajkonik*'s wooden mace.

St Adalbert and the Prussians

Dating back to the early 12th century, the tiny Romanesque **Kościół św Wojciecha** (St Adalbert's Church) looks as though it is sinking into the market square. The church, which resembles an elegant white cube with a Gothic cupola, is a small affair with room for only a few pews. Nevertheless, impressive interiors feature frescoes combining restraint and fully-fledged ornamentation. One such picture depicts St Adalbert being killed by the Prussians after he had baptised them in AD 997. It is believed that an earlier church on this site was the site of St Adalbert's last sermon before he set off with his missionaries to convert the Prussians. The poignant altar features gilded angels standing on either side of a painting of the Madonna and Child. The vaults house an exhibition (temporarily closed) of the History of Kraków's Market Square, with Romanesque and pre-Romanesque fragments of an even larger stone church, remnants of a wooden church believed to be the first in Kraków, and the wooden remains of an even earlier pagan temple.

In contrast with the diminutive St Adalbert's Church, the neighbouring church in the Main Market Square is the imposing, twin-towered **Kościół Mariacki** (St Mary's Church; ceremonial opening of the high altar, daily 11.50am). This church has two entrances, one for tourists (admission charged), the other for regular worshippers or those (excluding tourists) attending Mass. Construction

Above: St Adalbert's Church
Right: after a history of subjugation, Poles are free once again

of this triple-naved Gothic basilica began in 1290, incorporating fragments of an earlier Romanesque church that was burnt during the Tartar invasion of 1221. St Mary's was privately funded and, according to the medieval Polish chronicler Jan Długosz, it immediately became the city's principal parish church. The side chapels and towers were only completed in the early 14th century. The shorter of the two is the bell tower; the other, more ornamental tower bears a late-baroque 'crown' on the spire dedicated to the Virgin Mary, and served as a city watchtower.

The beautiful, monumental yet intricate interiors demand a leisurely visit for a full appreciation of the various architectural genres, including Gothic, Renaissance and Baroque. The late 19th-century polychromy was designed by the finest Polish artists, including Matejko and Stanisław Wyspiański, with stained glass windows also designed by Wyspiański and Józef Mehoffer.

The church's most extraordinary work of art is the late Gothic triptych altarpiece entitled *The Lives of Our Lady and Her Son Jesus Christ*. This was completed between 1477 and 1489 by the Nuremberg master carver Veit Stoss (known in Poland as Wit Stwosz), who was considered the finest craftsman of his age. The altarpiece incorporates 200 carved figures (many of them based on contemporary Cracovians) and decorative elements made from linden wood. The central panel, 13m (42ft) high and 11m (36ft) wide, depicts the Virgin Mary falling into an eternal sleep, surrounded by the apostles. Side panels depict scenes from the life of the Virgin Mary and Jesus, including the Annunciation, Resurrection, and Coronation of the Virgin Mary as Queen of Heaven. A Stwosz stone cross can be seen in the south aisle. After completing the cross and altarpiece, Stwosz remained in Kraków, where he worked for the king and aristocrats for a further 20 years.

Sounding the Trumpet

Every hour, on the hour, a trumpeter plays the *heynał*, a short tune, from the taller tower. This tradition originates in the time when a watchman, seeing the Tartars prepare to scale the city walls at dawn, blew his trumpet to raise the alarm. The Tartars fired a salvo of arrows at the watchman and, after a few notes, he was hit in the throat. It took some moments before a replacement took over, which explains why there is always a pause after the first few notes. Recently some students were caught trying to fleece tourists; pretending the *heynał* was played only at noon, they offered to arrange for it to be played on the next hour, for a fee.

Another local legend explains why the pigeons, which form such a prominent presence on the Main Market Square, originally arrived in the 13th century. Depending on whom you believe, either Duke Henryk Probus or Duke Władysław Łokietek were attempting to unify Poland's inde-

Left: St Mary's Church

pendent duchies and be proclaimed king. To secure papal support, the legendary duke had to visit the Vatican. He didn't have the funds for the trip so he sought the help of a notorious witch. She promised to lend him the money on condition that his retainers remained with her as a form of collateral. The witch then turned the retainers into pigeons. Travelling alone didn't suit the duke's sociable nature, so he made new friends and had fun. A lot of fun. Soon the gold was spent and when he returned to Kraków penniless, the witch refused to break the spell. She then vanished, leaving the duke's retainers as pigeons. This story explains why the pigeons are fondly considered to be noble rather than vermin, and those that come close to people are said to be the duke's retainers hoping to be told that the witch is finally going to be reimbursed.

Next to St Mary's Church on Plac Mariacki (Mariacki Square), laid out at the beginning of the 18th century on the site of the former parish cemetery, is **Kościół św Barbary** (St Barbara's Church). Apparently the church was constructed with the materials left from the construction of St Mary's Church, and by the same craftsmen. It originated in 1338 as the cemetery chapel, and sermons were given in Polish, in contrast with St Mary's Church, whose German-language sermons reflected the German dominance of the town council. King Zygmunt Stary (Sigismund the Old) reversed this in 1537.

Home of the Jesuits

St Barbara's was administered by the Jesuits from 1583 until 1773 when the order was dissolved in Poland. (It returned in 1874.) The small facade features a Renaissance portal as well as 15th-century late Gothic sculptures depicting Christ in the Olive Grove. The baroque interiors, effectively painted in two shades of blue, also include three Gothic works of sacral art – the *Pietà* sculpture, a crucifix, and polychromy depicting *The Apprehending of Christ*. Additional polychromy on the vaulted ceiling was completed by Piotr Franciszek Molitor in 1765. The 17th-century main altar has paintings of the Virgin Mary and St Barbara Lang (who died in 1621 and is buried in the crypt), as well as

Above: the trumpeter in St Mary's Church tower marks time

an exquisitely carved altar rail. The 17th-century Chapel of the Blessed Virgin Mary features the miraculous icon of Matka Boska Jurowicka (the Madonna of Jurowice), brought to Kraków in 1885 from the town of Jurowice where the cult of the Blessed Virgin Mary developed.

The **Mały Rynek** (Small Market Place) served as the city's meat market until the 19th century. A left turn brings you to the **Kamiennica Hipolytów** (Plac Mariacki 3, tel: 422 4219; open summer Wed–Sun 10am–5.30pm, Thur 10am–7pm; winter 9am–4pm, Thur 10am–7pm; closed 2nd Sun of every month; admission fee), a reconstruction of a wealthy burgher's house furnished in a 19th-century style.

Actors' Church

Taking ul Szpitalna, you'll find **Kościół sw Tomasza Apostoła** (Church of St Thomas the Apostle) at No 12. This is a prime example of 17th-century baroque architecture. Continuing along ul Szpitalna, you'll reach Plac św Ducha (The Holy Spirit's Square) where two definitive buildings of contrasting styles can be seen. The Gothic masterpiece **Kościół św Krzyża** (Holy Cross Church; ul św Krzyża 23) was established by the Duchaki Order of Preachers who arrived in Poland in 1222. The inner portal, the chapel of St Mary Magdalene and the baptismal font depicting scenes of the Annunciation, Crucifixion and various saints, are each wonderful examples of Gothic design. Moreover, a chapel dedicated to the founder of the church, St Dominic, is one of the best examples of Polish Renaissance art. The impressive vaulted ceiling, supported by a single pillar, includes 16th-century polychromy alongside 19th-century examples by Stanisław Wyspiański. An epitaph to the renowned 19th-century Polish actress Helena Modrzejewska, is one reason why this is also the unofficial actors' church, with a service dedicated to the city's thespians every Sunday.

Actors don't have far to go to attend this church – just across the square is one of the city's leading theatrical venues, the **Teatr im J Słowackiego** (Juliusz Słowacki Theatre; Plac św Ducha 1). This fabulously eclectic, neo-Renaissance confection was designed by Jan Zawiejski, who modelled it on the Paris Opera House. Built in 1893 on the site of a hospital originally run by the Duchaki Order, it features crimson and highly gilded interiors including impressive stage curtains painted with allegories of comedy and tragedy by Henryk Siemiradzki in 1892–94. The theatre screened the first film shown in Poland in 1896, and staged the premiere of Wyspiański's renowned *Wesele* (*The Wedding*) in 1901. The manicured flowerbeds laid out at the front of the theatre set off a bust of Aleksander Fredro, a hero of Polish comedy, sculpted by Cyprian Godebski.

Top: Czartoryski Museum. **Above:** adornment on Florian's Gate
Right: the small but fascinating Piarists' Church

Continue along ul Szpitalna, turn into ul Pijarska and you'll find **Brama Floriańska** (Florian's Gate). Having served as the principal entrance to the northern side of the city, this is the only remaining gateway of the town's medieval defensive system, which comprised eight gateways and almost 40 bastions. The gate's southern aspect features a royal Polish eagle of the Piast dynasty designed by Matejko. The passageway within the gate features a small, mid-19th century altar around a Gothic painting of Our Lady Mary of Piaski. A section of the historic city wall, together with four bastions dating from the 14th century, extend on either side of Florian's Gate. This wall now serves as open-air exhibition space for local painters (whose range covers the usual spectrum, from genuinely artistic to downright kitsch).

Illusory Murals

By the junction of ul Pijarów and ul św Jana is **Kościół Pijarów** (Piarists' Church), one of the city's smallest and most fascinating churches. The Piarist order first built a chapel and adjoining residence in Kraków in 1682, after the brothers had been asked to teach students of theology at the Jagiellonian University. The congregation grew to the extent that the chapel soon became too small, so Duke Hieronym Lubomirski acquired a neighbouring disused brewery for the Piarists. Wealthy Cracovians contributed to the building costs, and the new church was consecrated in 1759. But Francisco Placidi only finished the ornate facade in 1765.

The interiors feature Franciszek Eckstein and Jakub Hoffman's highly effective illusionistic murals, modelled on those of St Ignatius' Church in Rome. The vaulted ceiling and a depiction of Christ Ascending into Heaven (copied from Raphael) by the altar are particularly impressive. Side altars showcase the work of one of Poland's most talented 18th-century painters, Szymon Czechowicz, while the superb late-baroque sculptures are the work of Christian Boli.

Opposite the Piarists' Church is one of the city's most important museums, **Muzeum Czartoryskich** (Czartoryski Museum; ul św Jana 2; tel: 422 55 66; open May–Oct Tues, Thur 10am–4pm, Wed, Fri–Sat 10am–7pm, Sun 10am–3pm; Nov–Apr Tues, Thur, Sat–Sun 10am–3.30pm, Wed, Fri 10am–6pm; admission fee). This historic palace and neighbouring monastery were acquired by the Czartoryski family in 1876 to display their magnificent

art collection. The municipality donated the adjoining Renaissance arsenal to provide further galleries. These buildings offer a period setting for a fine collection that includes Polish and other European paintings, sculpture, sacral art and *objets d'art*, as well as ancient Roman, Greek and Egyptian art.

Among the highlights in the Painting Gallery, which features 13th- to 16th-century Polish, German, Italian, Spanish, Flemish and Dutch masters, are Rembrandt's *Landscape with a Merciful Samaritan* painted in 1638, and Leonardo da Vinci's *Lady with an Ermine* (1480–1490). This portrait,

thought to be of an Italian duke's mistress, was purchased by the Czartoryski family in 1800. A captivating, enigmatic painting, it hangs in its own room, where you can savour it while sitting on a specially provided bench.

Poland's First Cup of Coffee

The Tent Room's collection of Turkish effects was acquired at the Battle of Vienna in 1683, when King Jan III Sobieski led the victorious charge against the Ottoman aggressors. This exhibition includes a magnificent Turkish pavilion, suits of armour, various military items, and even coffee cups (the first coffee imbibed in Poland was taken from Turkish pavilions by the king). Among the ancient Roman, Etruscan and Greek collection are sculptures and busts, figurines, mosaics, vases, sarcophagi and papyrus fragments of books. The arsenal is used to stage temporary exhibitions.

Another church that's small in scale but large in significance is **Kościół św Jana Chrzciciela i św Jana Ewangelisty** (Church of St John the Baptist and St John the Evangelist; on the corner of ul św Jana 7 and ul św Tomasza). While the foundations and crypt of the original 12th-century Romanesque church have survived, the predominantly baroque characteristics derive from the 17th century. The baroque side altars in black and gold form a vivid contrast to the otherwise plain white interiors. Adjacent to the main altar is a painting of *Matka Bożej od Wykupu Niewolników* (Holy Mary Mother of God, of Releasing Prisoners of War) also known as *Matka Boska Wolności* (Holy Mary Mother of God of Liberty), which was donated by Duke Stanisław Radziwiłł – who acquired it in Spain – in about 1577.

Since the early 17th century, this painting has been associated with those Polish prisoners of war who were 'miraculously' freed after being sentenced to death by the Ottomans. The handcuffs of one such liberated prisoner still hang by the painting. King Jan III Sobieski, who defeated the Turks at the Battle of Vienna, subsequently prayed here in 1684 as a token of gratitude. An adjoining side chapel is dedicated to Matka Zofia Czeska (Mother Zofia Czeska, 1584–1650), the founder of the Order of Śióstr Prezentek (Sisters of St Thomas), which took over the administration of the church in 1726 and whose convent adjoins it. When you have finished viewing the church, continue along ul św Jana, which leads back to the Main Market Square.

Above: Church of St John the Baptist and St John the Evangelist

2. THE WAWEL ROYAL CASTLE *(see map, p33)*

A tour of Wawel Royal Castle and Cathedral, taking in the apartments that once accommodated Poland's kings, the treasury, armoury, chapels, crypt and bell tower, the museum and Dragon's Cave.

The castle complex is accessed via a cobbled route leading up Wawel Hill from Podzamcze. You emerge into a large square with the main ticket office to your right (purchase tickets for the cathedral from the office opposite the cathedral entrance). Visitor numbers are restricted and entry to some of Wawel's sites and museums operates on a timed basis. Note that tickets can sell out early in the day during peak season; to reserve in advance tel: 422 51 55

Wawel Castle and **Cathedral** tower over a 25-m (80-ft) high limestone hill overlooking the Wisła (Vistula) River. In the words of the artist Stanisław Wyspiański: 'Here everything is Poland, every stone and fragment, and the person who enters here becomes a part of Poland.'

The earliest traces of settlement on Wawel Hill date from the Palaeolithic age, 50,000 years ago. The earliest surviving architectural fragments, which include the earliest remains of a stone building in Poland – the pre-Romanesque rotunda of the Church of the Blessed Virgin Mary – are from the 10th century. Wawel Hill was established as the royal residence in 1038 when King Kazimierz Odnowiciel (Casimir the Restorer) transplanted the capital from Gniezno to Kraków and began building a royal residence. Under King Kazimierz Wielki (Casimir the Great, 1333–70) this evolved into a Gothic castle complex with defensive walls and towers that was subsequently extended by King Władysław Jagiełło (1386–1434).

The castle was ravaged by fire in 1499 but some of its Gothic elements, such as the Kurza Stopa

Above: the castle where 'everything is Poland'
Right: the castle courtyard

(Hen's Foot Tower), survived and were incorporated into a larger castle built by King Zygmunt Stary in 1504–36. He wanted a palatial residence and he certainly succeeded in creating one. The castle's perfectly proportioned, three-storey, arcaded courtyard is one of Europe's finest examples of Renaissance architecture. The designs were initiated by the Italian architect Francisco the Florentine and, in 1516, continued by another Italian architect, Bartolomeo Berrecci. The castle was finished in 1536 but subsequent fires meant refurbishment was required; in 1595, Giovanni Trevano introduced the early baroque elements and two additional towers.

Warsaw was declared the capital of Poland in 1596, and King Zygmunt III Waza (1587–1632) transferred the royal residence to Warsaw's Royal Castle in 1609. Though Wawel's importance was diminishing, it remained the site of the royal treasury and continued to hold coronations and royal funerals.

Invasion of the Swedes

The Wawel was ravaged and looted during the Swedish invasion of 1665–7, and the castle was torched by Swedish soldiers in 1702. In the 1780s, King Stanisław August Poniatowski commissioned his favourite architect, the Italian Dominik Merlini, to oversee the refurbishments, which incorporated the introduction of neoclassical elements. The partitions of Poland at the end of the 18th century saw the Prussians and then the Austrians loot the royal treasury. Austria turned the castle into a military barracks.

It wasn't until 1905 that Austrian troops left the castle and significant renovation work could be started. After numerous disputes, it was decided that, rather than trying to recreate the castle's Renaissance appearance, all of its various architectural styles should be restored. This work was still in progress when the Germans invaded in 1939. The main body of the castle had opened as a museum – with some sections serving as a presidential residence – when Poland regained independence in 1918. Many of the castle's treasures were shipped to Canada during the first few days of the invasion, thus denying the Nazis some handsome booty. Hans Frank, governor general of the puppet government subsequently established his headquarters within the Wawel. The entire castle and cathedral became a museum in 1945.

A tour of the **Royal Apartments** (open Apr–Oct Tues, Fri 9.30am–4pm, Wed, Thur, Sat 9.30am–3pm, Sun 10am–3pm; Nov–Mar Tues–Sat 9.30am–3pm, Sun 10am–3pm; admission fee) passes through various Renaissance and baroque apartments that feature wonderful interiors and works of art. Musicians in medieval costume occasionally add to the historic atmosphere.

Above: one of the castle's magnificent 16th-century arrases

The second floor accommodates the **State Rooms** (same opening hours as the Royal Apartments, also Apr–Oct 9.30am–noon; admission fee). The **Sala Poselska** (Parliamentary Hall) is also known as Sala pod Głowami (Hall under the Heads), because the wooden coffered ceiling is adorned with 30 sculpted heads, of kings, knights, burghers and allegorical and mythical figures. These include a gagged woman whose defence of an innocent woman accused of theft resulted in her release, on the king's order. The 30 heads are all that remain of the original 194 commissioned by Zygmunt Stary. Check out Dürer's frieze of scenes from the ancient world.

Royal portraits such as Rubens's *Elizabeth of Bourbon* (1629) hang in **Sala pod Orłem** (Hall under the Eagle), while **Sala Pod Ptakami** (Hall Under the Birds) features bird sculptures and a frieze that includes birds in its motifs. The walls of this magnificent room are covered in decoratively stamped leather and there's an impressive baroque marble fireplace dating from 1601. This is where King Zygmunt III Waza received foreign delegations – you can see the royal crest on a 17th-century wall hanging and on the stone portal.

Magnificent Wall Hangings

The castle's largest hall, **Sala Senatorska** (Senators' Hall), served as the senate's meeting place but official receptions and balls were also held here. It now displays an impressive arras entitled Cain Kills Abel. This is one of a magnificent collection of wall hangings – initially commissioned in the mid-16th century by King Zygmunt Stary and later by his son, King Zygmunt August – displayed throughout the castle. Produced in Brussels, the series is divided into three themes: Old Testament scenes; animals in exotic landscapes; and royal crests and insignia. Of the original 360 arrases, only 142 survived the Nazis.

The **Skarbiec i Zbrojownia** (Royal Treasury and Armoury Museum; open Apr–Oct Tues, Fri 9.30am–4pm, Wed, Thur, Sat 9.30am–3pm, Sun

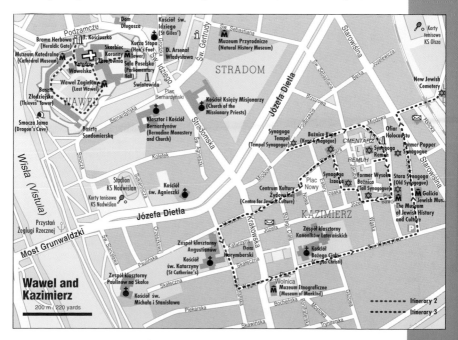

10am–3pm, Mon 9.30am–noon; Nov–Mar Tues–Sat 9.30am–3pm; admission fee) is housed in a Gothic section of the castle complete with vaulted ceilings. The 13th-century *szczerbiec* ('jagged sword') used at Polish coronations from 1320, is one of the most important exhibits of coronation regalia, royal jewels and medieval sacral art. Among the suits of armour and weapons are some ferocious double-handed swords, and the winged suits of armour worn by Polish hussars at the Battle of Vienna in 1683.

The **Wschód w Zbiorach Wawelskich** (The Orient in the Wawel Collections; open Apr–Oct Tues, Fri 9.30am–4pm, Wed, Thur, Sat 9.30am–3pm, Sun 10am–3pm; Nov–Mar Tues–Sat 9.30am–3pm; admission fee) brings together Turkish pavilions, armour, rugs and porcelain, some of which was taken as booty after the Battle of Vienna.

Dragon's Bones

As the scene of royal coronations, weddings, funerals and state occasions, the **Katedra Wawelska** (Wawel Cathedral; open May–Sept Tues–Sat 9am–5.15pm, Sun from 12.15pm; Oct–Apr 9am–3pm) is Poland's most

important church. A set of prehistoric bones by the entrance portal (designed by Trevano) has hung here for centuries. Local superstition holds that the bones are those of a dragon that inhabited a cave beneath the castle, from which it terrorised the city; only while the bones remain in place will the cathedral be safe. So far it has been. The scientific verdict links the 'dragon's bones' to prehistoric mammals.

The cathedral was built on the site of two Romanesque churches. It blends Gothic, Renaissance and baroque, but also has some Seccessionist stained-glass windows designed by Józef Mehoffer. The baroque main altar dates from the mid 17th century and features an emotive painting

Above: stained-glass window in Wawel Cathedral
Left: the cathedral blends architectural styles

of the Crucifixion. A total of 18 impressive side chapels dating from the 14th to 18th centuries include Kaplica Swieto Krzyska (Holy Cross Chapel), whose remarkable frescoes incorporate Ruthenian and Byzantine elements. But by far the most spectacular chapel, Kaplica Zygmuntowska (Sigismund's Chapel 1517–33), was designed by Santi Gucci, Padovano and Berreccio, and is regarded as one of the finest examples of Renaissance sacral art in Europe. Crowned by a magnificent gilded dome, using a mere 50kg (110lbs) of gold leaf, the chapel is the Jagiellonian dynasty's mausoleum. The tomb of King Zygmunt August is a masterpiece in red marble.

Set in a baroque altar dating from 1745, the Gothic Krzyż z Czarnym Chrystusem (Cross with the Black Christ) was brought to Poland by Queen Jadwiga, who left her native Hungary in 1384 aged 14. The queen prayed daily for hours at a time in front of the cross and it is said Christ spoke to her several times. She was canonised by Pope John Paul II in 1997 for her endless charitable work and for promoting Roman Catholicism in Poland. The royal tombs exemplify the finest craftsmanship down the ages. The earliest is the sarcophagus of King Władysław Łokietek (1333). The highly ornate tomb of St Stanisław, Poland's patron saint, with bas-reliefs on each side depicting his life, dates from 1671 and was sculpted in Gdańsk. The bishop was murdered in 1079 on the orders of King Boleslaus the Bold, who didn't appreciate the bishops criticisms of his immoral lifestyle.

Father Karol – Future Pope

Royal tombs can also be seen in the crypt, as well as those of renowned Poles such as the poets Adam Mickiewicz and Juliusz Słowacki, Tadeusz Kościuszko (who led the 1794 uprising during the partition of Poland), and the 20th-century statesman Marshal Józef Piłsudksi. This is usually far less crowded than the cathedral, which is frequently full of tour groups. The first section, known as St Leonard's Crypt, is a prime example of Romanesque style. This is where the newly-ordained Fr Karol Woytyła (subsequently Pope John Paul II) celebrated his first mass on November 2 1946. As Bishop of Kraków he presided over Wawel Cathedral for 10 years. Also in St Leonard's Crypt is the tomb of General Władysław Sikorski, prime minister of the Polish government in exile in World War II. He died in a helicopter crash off Gibraltar in 1943 and was buried in the Polish Armed Forces cemetery in Newark, England. In accordance with his wish to be buried in an independent Poland, his remains were ceremonially laid to rest here in 1993.

The remarkable Dzwon Zygmunta (Sigismund's Bell) is in the cathedral's **Wieża Zygmuntowska** (Sigismund's Tower). Cast in 1520 and hung the next

Right: inside the cathedral

year, the bell weighs 18 tons. It's the largest bell in Poland, and is rung only on special occasions. The climb up the tower's steep, cramped staircase is hard work, but the bell is definitely worth seeing. According to local superstition, you should touch the bell's clapper with your left hand and your wish will be granted. There are also fabulous views over the historic centre from the tower.

Opposite the cathedral entrance, a separate building houses the **Muzeum Katedralne** (Cathedral Museum; open Tues–Sun 10am–3pm; admission fee), an initiative of the pope when he was Bishop of Kraków. Here you can see 12th- to 18th-century sacral art, rugs, votive offerings and religious relics, particularly those associated with St Stanisław and Pope John Paul II.

Housed within the former royal kitchens and coach house, **Wawel Zaginiony** (Lost Wawel; open Apr–Oct Tues, Fri 9.30am–4pm, Wed, Thur, Sat 9.30am–3pm, Sun 10am–3pm, Mon 9.30am–noon; Nov–Mar Mon, Wed–Sat 9.30am–3pm, Sun 10am–3pm; admission fee) includes archaeological and architectural remains, such as decorative Gothic tiles and the poignant rotunda of the Church of the Blessed Virgin Mary, one of the earliest buildings on Wawel Hill. Stroll around the Wawel grounds for a closer look at the 15th- to 16th-century defensive walls as well as some medieval ruins. And check out the equestrian statue of Tadeusz Kościuszko (1920) by the Brama Herbowa (Heraldic Gate, 1920).

Smocza Jama (Dragon's Cave; open daily 10am–5pm May–Oct) is thought to be one of several under Wawel Hill and has been the scene of many a licentious episode. In the 19th century it housed a brothel, until the Austrian authorities bricked up the cave entrance. The visitor's entrance is on Wawel Hill, where you'll find the ticket office too. At the exit to the cave, a metal sculpture of a slim, 1960s-style dragon periodically breathes gas flames. By the Wawel, on Bulwar Czerwiński (tel: 422 08 55) you can join boat trips along the Vistula.

King Krak

The legend of the dragon has numerous variations. One constant theme finds the dragon awoken from a deep sleep by the noise of the castle's builders. Venturing out for food, the dragon devoured beautiful virgins, handsome young men, and any creature that strayed close to the cave. Or it might have consumed only the beautiful virgins. Some versions claim that King Krak delivered his people from the dragon, others that he sought a volunteer – promising half the kingdom, and his daughter's hand in marriage – to slay the beast. Many knights tried and failed. Eventually a shoemaker left a sheep's carcas filled with sulphur and salt by the cave entrance. Either the contents of the sheep made the dragon so thirsty that it drank river water till it burst, or the sheep blew up inside it. The shoemaker married the princess and they lived happily ever after.

Above: the 18-tonne Sigismund's Bell, dating to 1520, is the largest in the country
Right: cafés in Szeroka Street in the Jewish district of Kazimierz

3. THE JEWISH QUARTER *(see map, p33)*

**Explore Kazimierz, the historic Jewish district of Kraków, taking in
an array of synagogues from different periods, the Museum of Judaism
and other cultural centres, and a host of Jewish cafés and restaurants.**

*Kazimierz is easy to reach from the Main Market Square – walk along ul
Grodzka, then take ul Stradomska and turn into ul Miodowa*

Kazimierz was founded as a town in its own right just outside Kraków by
King Kazimierz Wielki (Casimir the Great), who gave the town his own
name, in 1335. Although Kazimierz is known as a centre of Jewish life, it
was not totally so – the district has several historic Roman Catholic churches.
The Jewish nature of Kazimierz dates back to 1494 and King Jan Olbracht's
expulsion of Kraków's Jewish population. Many settled in Kazimierz, to
which they were followed by other persecuted Jews from across Europe.

Commerce thrived and, by the 16th century, the town's Jewish community
was one of the most prominent in Europe. Indeed the renowned Talmudic
scholar and philosopher Rabbi Moses Isserles (known as Remuh) founded
his academy here. Kazimierz became a walled town, complete with gateways, town hall and marketplace in the early 17th century. Only in 1800,
when this part of Poland was annexed by the Austro-Hungarian Empire,
was Kazimierz incorporated into Kraków.

Oskar Schindler

When Germany invaded Poland in September 1939, about 70,000 Jews
lived in Kazimierz, most of whom were soon 'resettled' in other parts of
the country. In 1941 the Nazis established a Jewish ghetto in Podgórze, a separate district of Kraków, into which they herded Kazimierz's remaining
20,000 Jews. From here they were sent to either Auschwitz or Płaszów.
The latter, initially a slave labour camp, served as a concentration camp
from 1944. Only about 1,000–2,000 of Kazimierz's prewar Jewish population
survived the Nazis; today about 100 Jews live in the district. Some were saved
from almost certain death by Oskar Schindler, who employed them as slave
labour in his factory. Schindler's story was the subject of Thomas Keneally's

book *Schindler's Ark*, on which Steven Spielberg based his Oscar-winning film *Schindler's List*. Unlike so many of the continent's centres of Jewish life, Kazimierz survived – the Nazis planned to establish a macabre museum of what were termed 'vanished races' in this area.

At the junction with ul Podbrzezie you'll find the Reform (as opposed to Orthodox) Jewish congregation's **Tempel Synagogue** (ul Miodowa 24; open Mon–Fri, Sun 10am–4pm; admission fee). This synagogue was built in 1862, and extended on both sides in 1924. Of the few houses of Jewish prayer in Kazimierz that survived the Nazi regime virtually intact, this was the newest. Whereas the facade combines neo-Renaissance with Moorish influences, the dazzling interiors blend beautifully ornate stucco work, intricate red-and-gold polychromy, and a set of four circular stained-glass windows by the altar closet. Above highly gilded galleries on both sides, the beautiful ceiling is decorated with gold stars on a light blue background. An exhibition area includes photographs and architectural drawings of all the synagogues in Kazimierz, together with historical details. Across the road, beyond a courtyard, you can see the rear elevation of the 17th-century **Bożnica Kupa** (Kupa Synagogue). The front of this recently restored building is on ul J Warszauera.

Nostalgic Tunes

Turn into ul Szeroka ('Wide Street') and you will be in what was once Kazimierz's centre of Jewish life and commerce. There was a time when this quiet neighbourhood was the most prestigious residential street inhabited by the wealthiest Jews. The current restoration work is preserving its Jewish character. Growing numbers of visiting tourists take 'Oskar Schindler tours', and wandering troubadors play nostalgic tunes in Szeroka's Jewish cafés and restaurants.

The substantial **Landau's House** (at No 2), was built as a manor house in the 16th century by the wealthy magnate and Kazimierz worthy Spytk Jordan. Overlooking a small green, it now houses the Jarden bookshop, which stocks a good range of guide books. Check out the attractive, 1920s-

style decor of the Noah's Ark café and, if you fancy expert accompaniment to your visit, this is the place to book local Jewish guides for walking tours of the area. Also dating from the 16th century, the Klezmer-Hois Hotel (No 6) occupies a building that used to house the *mikve* (ritual baths).

The **Popper Synagogue**, approached through a courtyard at No 16, was founded in 1620 by Wolf Popper, a wealthy merchant and financier also known as Bocian ('Stork'). Originally decorated and furnished in a lavish style, it was destroyed by the Nazis and is currently utilised as a cultural centre.

Working your way back up the opposite side of the street, the smallest synagogue in Kazimierz, **Remuh** (ul Szeroka 40; open

Left: Tempel Synagogue

Mon–Fri 9am–4pm; admission fee), is not merely a historic monument: it remains the centre of the neighbourhood's Jewish life and has an active, albeit small, congregation. Remuh, which dates from 1553, was the town's second synagogue, and was originally known as the 'New Synagogue'. The founder, Israel ben Joseph, was a merchant and banker to King Zygmunt Stary, and the father of the renowned rabbi and philosopher Remuh (1525–72).

Approach the synagogue via a small, irregular courtyard and you'll see a harmonious blend of architectural genres. The current appearance dates from the major refurbishment of the 1880s and the postwar reconstruction.

A rectangular, single-aisle hall is overlooked by a women's gallery. The stone money box by the entrance to the prayer room dates from the 17th century, while the altar features a plaque commemorating the spot where Rabbi Remuh prayed, and there are Renaissance stone portal and Seccessionist doors. Caramel-coloured walls provide a background for fragments of period tiles with classical motifs, and a few early 20th-century wall paintings depict Noah's Ark, the grave of the biblical matriarch Rachel and Jerusalem's 'Wailing' Wall.

Renaissance Cemetery

There's also a 'wailing' Wall in the adjoining cemetery, on the ul Szeroka side. This was built with fragments of Nazi-desecrated tombstones that were too small to be reconstructed. This, one of only two Renaissance Jewish cemeteries in Europe (the other is in Prague), was laid out in the 1530s and was active until the early 19th century. Some 700 tombstones, including ornate Renaissance and baroque examples, fill 4.5ha (11 acres).

If you're ready for a coffee or lunch break **Alef** (No 17; tel: 421 3870) has a delightful, *fin-de-siècle* townhouse atmosphere and live Jewish music.

Above: the historic Remuh cemetery dates back to the 1530s
Right: art students make the most of Kazimierz's atmosphere

The neighbouring **Ariel restaurant** (No 18; tel: 421 79 20) is less bohemian, but has pavement tables and an attractive patio garden with goldfish pool.

Poland's oldest surviving synagogue, **Stara Synagoga** (Old Synagogue; ul Szeroka 24; tel: 422 09 62; open Apr–Oct Mon 10am–2pm, Tues–Sun 10am–5pm; Nov–Mar Wed, Thur, Sat, Sun 9am–4pm, Mon 10am–2pm, Fri 10am–5pm; admission fee) is home to the Museum of Jewish History and Culture. Dating from the early 15th century, this building was partly modelled on synagogues in Prague, Regensburg and Worms, which explains the Gothic facade. It was extended in the 16th century, when the architect Matteo Gucci of Florence introduced the synagogue's Renaissance elements. In the following

century, a women's prayer room and a meeting hall for the Jewish Community Council were established on the first floor. Demolition work in 1880 revealed some of the synagogue's original walls. Based on this discovery, reconstruction combined the original style with neo-Renaissance elements. The rebuilding process continued until the early 20th century; the synagogue remained the centre of Jewish worship in Kazimierz until the Nazi invasion. The Nazis used it as a warehouse before destroying the interiors and roof. It wasn't until several years after the war that the ruins were reconstructed. The synagogue re-opened as a museum in 1958.

Museum of Jewish History and Culture

The museum's extensive collection provides such good explanations of the Jewish faith, its history and culture that, even if you have little prior knowledge, it is easy to understand the significance of each exhibit. Numerous religious items were collected from other synagogues. The main picture gallery includes portraits by the renowned painter Józef Mehoffer, whereas the gallery on the first floor features 19th- and early 20th-century views of Kazimierz. An exhibition of Jewish life in Kazimierz 1939–45 displays original photographs and documents that trace the course of the Nazi regime, taking in the ghetto and subsequent transports to concentration camps.

A monument in front of the museum marks the site where 30 Jews were executed by the Nazis in 1943; to the right is the former Na Górce Synagogue. Although the name's literal translation is 'Synagogue on the Hill', it actually means 'Upper Synagogue', signifying that the prayer hall was on the first floor (the ground floor housed a *mikve*). This synagogue was known for its connection with Natan Spira, who lectured across Europe on the practice of *Kabbala* (a mystical means of understanding the Old Testament).

Continue to ul Józefa and you will find the former **Wysoka Bożnica** (Tall Synagogue; No 38), dating from the mid-16th century and restored after its destruction by the Nazis in 1939. The facade features a Renaissance portal and four elegant buttresses. As at Na Górce, the prayer hall was on the first floor. The building now houses a branch of the city's conservation department.

Take ul Jakuba (Jacob's Street), which leads directly to ul Izaaka (Isaac's Street). The latter was named after Yitzhok ben Yekeles (Isaac, son of Jacob),

Above: advertising an exhibition on Polish Jewry at the Isaac Synagogue
Right: the Isaac Synagogue is one of the oldest in Kazimierz

one of 17th-century Kazimierz's wealthiest merchants and moneylenders and founder of the Isaac Synagogue on the corner of ul Izaaka and ul Kupa. The story behind his fabulous wealth, now a common fable in Jewish folk lore, is entertainingly recounted by Rabbi Symcha Bunam from Przysucha, who was a leading figure in Chassidic Jewry. Isaac, a pious, God-fearing and impoverished man, was told in a dream that treasure hidden under an old bridge in Prague was destined to be his. Inspired, he set off for the great city on foot – he couldn't afford a more luxurious means of transport.

The Moral of Hidden Treasure

He reached Prague but was disappointed to find the bridge guarded. So, deciding to share the treasure with the soldiers in return for their help, he told them of his dream. An officer replied dismissively that he had also dreamt about treasure, hidden in an oven in the home of a poor Kazimierz Jew called Isaac son of Jacob, but that this would not induce him to travel all the way to Kazimierz in search of it. Foiled, Isaac returned home. Recalling the officer's dream, he dismantled his oven and, lo and behold, there was the treasure. Isaac used the treasure to fund numerous good deeds. When neighbours enquired about the source of his wealth, Isaac replied: 'There are things you may look for all over the world, and yet find in your own home. But before you realise this, you usually have to travel far and wide.'

Ceremoniously inaugurated in 1644, the **Isaac Synagogue** (ul Kupa 18; open Mon–Fri, Sun 9am–7pm; admission fee) is the largest synagogue in Kazimierz, and was, in contrast with its current 'minimalist' interiors, also the most lavishly furnished. Ravaged by the Nazis, the building served as a sculptor's workshop after the war and it wasn't until 1983 that renovation work began.

Nevertheless, the baroque prayer hall retains a distinctive beauty and features fragments of recently uncovered 17th-century wall murals together with some stucco decoration by Jean Baptiste Falconi. On the east wall is a stone altar tabernacle *(aron hakodesh)*; the women's gallery *(ezrat nashim)* features an elegant arcade of Tuscan columns. Cardboard figures represent rabbis and a

small television screens a short historical film about the Jews of Kazimierz. In another part of the synagogue, adjoining a photographic exhibition of prewar life entitled 'The Memory of Polish Jews', you can see a film by the American Julian Bryan that traces the history of Jewish life in Kraków and Kazimierz.

From Generation to Generation

Turn into ul Warszauera, continue past the front elevation of Bożnica Kupa (Kupa Synagogue) and into **Plac Nowy** (New Square). A small, circular building occupies its centre which on closer inspection reveals the tiled interior of the old fruit and vegetable market. This buzzing square with its scattering of bric-à-brac and hot food stalls has been revived by an influx of bohemian cafés and sleek, low-lit bars but retains an edgy individuality. Cross over to the **Centrum Kultury Żydowskiej** (Judaica Foundation, Centre for Jewish Culture; ul Meiselsa 17; tel: 430 6449; open Mon–Fri 10am–6pm, Sat, Sun 10am–2pm).

Established in 1993 and concealed behind the 1886 period facade of the former B'ne Emuna prayer house, the centre hosts conferences, seminars and movies and documentaries relating to Jewish culture. The centre's motto, *L'dor v'dor* (Hebrew for 'from generation to generation'), emphasises its commitment to Jewish continuity after the Holocaust. The well-stocked information desk provides details of the annual Festival of Jewish Culture. The centre also incorporates a workshop, an art gallery, a bookshop that sells antique books and postcards, and a café.

Continue along ul Meiselsa and turn into ul Augustiańska, which leads to **Kościół św Katarzyny** (St Catherine's Church; No 7). This prime example of Gothic architecture was founded by King Kazimierz Wielki in 1363, apparently as a form of penance for sentencing Fr Marcin Baryczyk to death by drowning in the River Vistula. This was a classic case of shooting the messenger: the priest had committed the heinous crime of conveying the bishop's disapproval of the king's dalliances with various mistresses.

The church's interiors include baroque details, such as the particularly impressive altar. The cloisters of the adjoining Augustinian monastery feature remarkable frescoes from the 14th and 15th centuries. An altar dedicated to Matka Boska Pocieszenia (Our Lady the Comforter) dates from the early 15th century, and was one of the most important sites in Poland's cult of the Virgin Mary.

Museum of Mankind

Continue along ul Weglowa to Plac Wolnica, the former marketplace of Kazimierz, overlooked by the **Muzeum Etnograficzne** (Museum

Left: Museum of Jewish History and Culture in the Old Synagogue

of Mankind; Pl Wolnica 1; tel: 430 55 75; entrance on ul Krakowska 46; open Mon 10am–6pm, Wed–Fri 10am–3pm, Sat, Sun 10am–2pm; admission fee). This is housed in a splendid early-15th century building that served as the ratusz (town hall) of Kazimierz until 1800 and which was continually extended and restyled until the mid-19th century.

The museum was founded in 1947 and features an extensive collection of folk arts and crafts drawn from villages in the regions of Kraków, Podhale and Silesia. These take the form of paintings, sculpture and costumes, as well as naive sacral art and Christian exhibits such as Nativity cribs and Easter eggs painted with rustic motifs. Re-created interiors featuring authentic period furniture and decor are redolent of traditional village homes. The collection extends beyond Poland, with rarities such as late 19th-century Siberian fur coats and folk costumes from Belarus and the Ukraine.

Casimir the Great takes the credit for founding yet another of Kraków's most beautiful Gothic churches, **Kościół Bożego Ciała** (Church of Corpus Christi; ul Bożego Ciała 26). The reason behind the establishment of the church at this particular location is an interesting one: apparently it was here that thieves fleeing from the clutches of their pursuers abandoned a monstrance containing the Eucharistic host, which they had stolen from the Kościół Wszystkich Świętych (All Saints' Church), which featured prominently in central Kraków until the 19th century.

Building work began in 1340, but it wasn't completed until late in the 14th century, when it became the parish church for Roman Catholics living in Kazimierz. At the start of the 15th century, King Władysław Jagiełło invited the canons of the Lateran Order to supervise the church – their residences can still be seen across the courtyard by the entrance. Among the Gothic, Renaissance and baroque elements of this ornate but dignified church is the Renaissance tombstone of Bartolomeo Bereccio, who co-designed Sigismund's Chapel, and the Gothic stained-glass windows, in Wawel Cathedral. The gilded main altar, dating from the 1630s, includes a painting of the Nativity Scene by Tomasz Dolabela, while the ornamental pulpit takes the form of a boat.

Continue along ul św Wawrzynca, turning left into ul Dajwór, where the **Galicia Jewish Museum** is located at no 18 (tel: 421 6842; open daily 9am–7pm, admission fee). This photographic exhibition covers Jewish life in Polish Galicia, and the centre additionally hosts Yiddish and Hebrew language courses, concerts and more. Turn right into ul Miodowa and walk beyond the viaduct to reach the **New Jewish Cemetery** at No 55. The cemetery, established at the beginning of the 19th century, contains the graves of many renowned Jews.

Above: the Museum of Mankind occupies the former town hall on Plac Wolnica

4. THE NATIONAL MUSEUM *(see map below)*

A morning visit to the National Museum, the city's largest and most comprehensive, and the surrounding area west of the historic centre.

Don't be discouraged by the unattractive, 1930s modernist architecture of the **Muzeum Narodowe** (National Museum; al 3 Maja 1; tel: 295 5500; open Tues, Thur, Sun 10am–3.30pm, Wed, Fri, Sat 10am–6pm; admission fee, permanent exhibitions). Inside, an array of historic works of art is well-organised in a number of galleries. The Arms and Uniforms Gallery displays an extensive collection of military exhibits, ranging from the Middle Ages to the 20th century, including poignant memorabilia of the 18th- and 19th-century rebellions against partition. The World War II collection features military decorations and medals.

Also covering the Middle Ages to the 20th century, the arts and crafts in the Gallery of Decorative Arts detail Kraków's history as the country's centre of fine art. Here you'll find silver and golds items, sacral art, clocks, glass and a collection of ceramics that spans Polish and European decorative tiles, faïence and porcelain, with examples by Meissen and Sevres. Polish furniture, particularly from Gdańsk, is well represented in a series of rooms that highlights such genres as Biedermier, Empire and Secessionist. The 20th-Century Polish Art and Sculpture Gallery is one of the country's most comprehensive collections. More than 600 exhibits extend from the *Młoda Polska* ('Young Poland') movement that pioneered Secessionism (Stanisław Wyspiański, Wojciech Weiss, Józef Mehoffer) through the avant-garde Kraków Group of the early 20th century, to modern and contemporary art by the likes of the Expressionist Stanisław Witkiewicz.

Neighbouring the museum, and also accessible from al 3 Maja, are the large Park dr H Jordana, named after a renowned 19th-century Cracovian

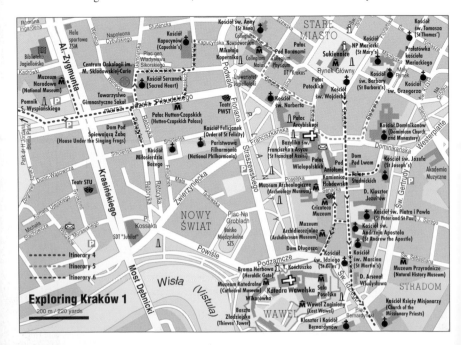

city itineraries

doctor, and the vast Błonia meadow, which provide a welcome green touch.

On the adjoining ul Marszała Piłsudskiego (named after the states-man and inter-war army commander) you'll find **Towarzystwo Gimnasty-czne 'Sokół'** at No 27, the gymnasium of an organisation founded in 1867 to promote physical fitness. This was actually a cover for the military train-ing of Kraków's youth during the period of partitions. Opened in 1889, it's the city's oldest gym. Whereas the late 19th-century facade features neo-Gothic elements, the ornamental friezes incorporate graffiti decorations.

On the corner of ul Piłsudskiego and ul Retoryka is **Dom Pod Śpiewa-jącą Żabą** (House Under the Singing Frog). Designed by Teodor Talowski, it is a prime example of the neigh-bourhood's 'historic revival' architecture. Neighbouring buildings at ul Piłsudskiego 30, 32, 34 and 36 are eclectic Secessionism. Turning into ul Retoryka, numbers 3, 7 and 9 are Talowski creations from 1887–91. Avoid even looking at the bland modern blocks on the other side of the road.

Coins and Notes

The Hutten-Czapski family bequeathed the late 19th-century neo-Renaissance **Pałac Hutten-Czapskich** (Hutten-Czapskich Palace; ul Marszała Piłsud-skiego 12; tel: 422 27 33; admission for research by prior arrangement only) to the National Museum in 1902. It houses a fine collection of historic coins and notes. At No 16 is the attractive, neoclassical build-ing where the novelist Henryk Sienkiewicz, who won the Nobel Prize for literature in 1905, often stayed. There aren't many cafés hereabouts, but cross the road and you can stop for a coffee in the Hotel Fortuna (entrance in ul Czapskich 5).

Heading up to ul Garncarska, **Kościół Najświętszego Serca** (Church of the Sacred Heart; No 26) presents a typical combination of a neo-Gothic facade fea-turing a bas-relief of the Madonna and Child and neo-Renaissance and Seces-sionist interiors. The church is the centre of the cult of St Jozef Sebastian Pelczar, a distinguished 19th-century Kraków University theologian. Pope John Paul II prayed beside the tomb when he visited the church in 1991.

Now turn into ul Jabłonoskich, then into ul Loretańska. **Kościół**

Above: on display in the National Museum's Arms and Uniforms Gallery
Right: the museum's modernist exterior gives no hint of the exhibits' antiquity

Kapucynów (Capuchin's Church; Loretańska 11) was commissioned by the Capuchin order late in the 18th century in accordance with its vow of poverty – hence its particularly pronounced air of modesty. Side chapels dedicated to the Sacred Heart of Jesus, and the Crucified Christ, are nevertheless deeply moving, and the church's important paintings include the *Annunciation* by Pietro Dandini. Cloisters link the church to the early 18th-century neoclassical Chapel of Santa Loreto. Based on the Casa Santa Loreto in Italy – itself a replica of the house in which the Annunciation took place – this chapel houses the figure of The Madonna of Loreto. Jan Bukowski's Secessionist polychromy dates from 1925. A statue of St Francis of Assisi, who formulated the principles of the Capuchin order in 1221, stands by the church entrance. The church is, incidentally, renowned for its annual Christmas crib.

5. HISTORIC COLLEGES *(see map, p44)*

Visit some of the the Jagiellonian University's historic colleges, including Collegium Maius and Collegium Nowodworski, and two of the city's most imposing churches, the Franciscan and the Dominican.

For a truly flamboyant example of baroque style, begin at **Kościół św Anny** (St Anna's Church; ul św Anny 11). Modelled on Rome's Church of St Andrew della Valle by Tylman of Gameren, who designed many of Poland's most beautiful baroque structures, St Anna's was built as the university church between 1689 and 1703. The earliest reference to a church on this site dates from 1381. After that was destroyed by a fire in 1407, its successor was a Gothic church funded by King Władysław Jagiełło. Extended in 1428, it gained collegiate status in 1535, but was demolished in 1689, having become too small for the congregation. This was partly due to the growing cult of St Jan Kanty, whose tomb is to the right of the main altar. A theology professor at the Jagiellonian University, Kanty was canonised in 1775.

The degree of ornamentation throughout the church is intense but always ethereally light, with majestic frescoes, particularly in the cupola. Sculptures (including one of St Anna herself) and magnificent stucco designs featuring fruit and floral motifs are the work of the Italian Baltazar Fontana. The 17th-century painting of St Anna on the main altar is by King Jan III Sobieski's court painter, Jerzy Siemiginowski.

Across the road is **Collegium Nowodworskie** (Nowodworksi College; ul św Anny 12), which was founded as a grammar school in 1588 by Bartłomiej Nowodworksi, one of the king's private secretaries. The present building, the university's Collegium Medicum, complete with arcaded courtyard, dates from 1643 and is the oldest Polish college still in use.

Now a museum, **Collegium Maius** (Maius College; ul Jagiellońska 15; tel: 422 05 49; open Mon–Fri 10am–3pm, Thur till 6pm, Sat 11am–3pm; admission fee to museum) was Poland's first university college

Left: sculpture by Baltazar Fontana, St Anna's Church

city itineraries

(and the second in central and eastern Europe after Prague). This college originated in Wawel Castle in 1364. In 1400 King Władysław Jagiełło purchased a house on what is now Jagiełłonska Street from a wealthy merchant family called Pęcherz to serve as the seat of the college, then known as Academia Krakóviensis. The house was soon extended and neighbouring houses were acquired and linked by annexes. These buildings burnt down in the late 15th century, and a purpose-built college with an elegant Gothic facade took their place. Completed in 1492, when it became known as Collegium Maius, it included the stunning arcaded cloister, from which 'professors' staircases' lead up to the professorial chambers on the first and second floors. It was refurbished in a neo-Gothic style during the 19th century, with the original Gothic appearance restored between 1949 and 1964.

The professors' common room, the treasury, assembly hall and library were built in 1507–19 in Gothic style. The library features a beautifully painted skyscape on the vaulted ceiling, as well as historic portraits and various rare tomes – it became the university library in 1860. The former professors' dining room has distinctive Gdańsk cupboards and an extensive collection of gold and silver tableware.

Copernicus

The Mikołaj Kopernik Room commemorates the life of the renowned astronomer Nicolas Copernicus, who studied here in 1491–95. His then revolutionary theory that the sun and not the earth was the centre of the universe, and that the earth and planets revolved around the sun was set forth in *De Revolutionibus Orbium Coelestium*, which he completed in 1530 after studying in Bologna, Padua and Rome.

Above: Nowodworskie College dates back to 1588
Right: Maius College is now a museum

His work provided a foundation for subsequent theories by astronomers such as Galileo. Hand-written sections of the original manuscript can be seen in the Copernicus Room, together with a collection of historic portraits, astrolabes (navigational aids that measure the altitude of stars and the planets) and other such astronomical instruments from the 1480s. A 1510 golden globe, one of the first to show the New World, bears the inscription, '*America, terra noviter reperta*' ('America, a newly discovered land'). The walls of the *aula* (assembly hall) feature more than 100 paintings, including portraits of King Władysław Jagiełło and his wife Queen Jadwiga.

Entrance to the courtyard is free whenever the college is open, and there's a good souvenir shop just off the courtyard. Admission to the museum is only as part of a guided tour (tickets from the ground-floor office in the courtyard).

Turn into ul Gołębia, then right into ul Bracka, leading to **Bazylika św Francziszka z Asyżu** (Basilica of St Francis of Assisi; entrance from ul Francziszkańska 1, or Plac Wszystkich Swiętych 5). Striking in its imposing beauty, this church was founded for the Franciscan order, which arrived in Kraków in 1222 at the invitation of King Bolesław Wstydliwy (Boleslaus the Bashful), who is buried here. Designed in the form of a Greek cross, and built in a Gothic style between 1252 and 1269, it was greatly extended during the 15th century.

The great fire of Kraków in 1850 destroyed some historic features and resulted in further rebuilding in a neo-Gothic style. But the church has retained historic elements such as the Gothic galleries and fragments of wall paintings in the adjoining Franciscan monastery. By the baroque altar, the apse features a Tadeusz Popiel mosaic depicting St Francis of Assisi. Kaplica Matki Boskiej Bolesnej (Chapel of Our Lady the Sorrowful), itself the size of a small church, has a 15th-century painting of the Madonna, and fine polychromy.

A Truly Spiritual Experience

The church showcases the work of two of the country's greatest Secessionist artists. The paintings representing the Stations of the Cross are by Józef Mehoffer, while the stunning polychromy on the walls and vaulted ceilings was designed by Stanisław Wyspiański. The effect of this intense combination of Gothic and floral motifs with Secessionist elements is dazzling, though

Above: a stunning depiction of The Creation at the Basilica of St Francis of Assisi

it can take a little time to appreciate while you adjust your eyes to the church's sombre lighting. Paradoxically, the semi-darkness heightens the beauty of the stained-glass windows, also designed by Wyspiański. For a genuinely spiritual experience, stand in the main nave and look up at the most important of these windows, over the main entrance. The lilac-and-blue palette, completed in 1900, is an astonishing depiction of the Creation.

The next extraordinary ecclesiastical centre is just across the square. The Basilica of the Holy Trinity; more commonly known as **Kościół Dominikanów** (the Dominican Church and monastery; ul Stolarska 12), is as august and austere as the Franciscan church, although the building represents a very different tradition. Its character is immediately indicated by the highly geometric, neo-Gothic facade.

Chapel of St Dominic

The church originated in 1222, when the Dominicans reached Poland. The first, Romanesque, church, destroyed by the Tartars in 1241, was greatly extended during the 15th century, when Renaissance elements were added. The Chapel of St Dominic, who founded the order in Italy, is one of the most beautiful examples of Renaissance art in the country. The renovations that followed the great fire of 1850 introduced neo-Gothic elements. Of the architectural genres that have survived, fragments of original Gothic can be seen in the Chapel of St Mary Magdalene and tombstones completed by Wit Stwosz.

The rococo Kaplica Matki Boskiej Różancowej (Chapel of Our Lady of the Rosary), dating from 1685, contains a painting of the Madonna copied from the Our Lady of the Rosary painting in the Basilica of St Maria Maggiore in Rome. This chapel and painting are linked to the Polish victory over the Turks in the Battle of Vienna in 1683. The Kaplica św Jacka (Chapel of St Hyacinth) features this saint's ornamental baroque tomb, with surrounding stucco work designed by Baltazar Fontana. St Hyacinth, who died in 1257, founded the Dominican Order in Poland. You can also see the cloisters in the adjoining Dominican monastery, where many of the city's most illustrious residents were laid to rest.

The adjoining ul Stolarska, which extends to the edge of the Small Market Square, was named after the carpenters who traditionally plied their trade in workshops here. A wooden arcade on one side of the street (Nos 8–10) features various specialist shops, including a travel agent, a jeweller's, an antiquarian bookshop selling old maps and prints and, displaying graphic art exhibited at the city's foremost art shows, the Galeria Plakatu (Poster Gallery). The grand buildings on the other side of the road house the French, German and American consulates.

Above: cloisters at the Dominican Church

6. TWO HISTORIC THOROUGHFARES *(see map, p44)*

The historic ul Grodzka combines imposing town houses, august institutions and stunning churches; the adjoining ul Kanoniczna, one of the city's most exquisite streets, is home to several museums.

The long and beautiful ul Grodzka, a main thoroughfare that leads from the Main Market Square to Wawel Castle, comprises a fascinating mixture of restaurants, cafés and bars, shops and galleries. Its origins actually pre-date Kraków's town charter (1257) – it was probably established as a principal street in the 9th century. Ul Grodzka was traditionally known as Droga Solna (The Salt Road) because it heads off towards the Wieliczka and Bochnia salt mines.

Among the most attractive houses, **Dom Pod Lwem** (House Under the Lion) at No 32 has a 14th-century stone lion carved above the portal. **Pod Aniołami** (Under the Angels) at No 35 is a delightful Polish restaurant and café with an atmospheric vaulted cellar decorated in a folksy style and a charming patio garden. At No 38, **Dom Pod Elefanty** (House Under the Elephants) is thought to have been the residence and premises of Bonifazio Cantelli, a 17th-century royal apothecary. The exotic animals depicted on the facade formed a typical apothecary's sign – not to be confused with the golden elephant at No 11 Plac Wszystkich Świętych. **Dom Wit Stwosza** (Wit Stwosz's House) at No 39–41 was the residence of the master carver from Nuremberg from 1478 to 1492.

Turn into ul Poselska and at No 21 you'll find the baroque Kosciół św Józefa (St Joseph's Church) and the adjoining Bernardine Convent. The Jagiellonian University's **Collegium Iuridicum** (ul Grodzka 53), which dates from the 15th century, was restyled and extended in the 16th century. This college houses the university's history of art faculty and, beyond an attractive baroque portal, features an arcaded courtyard.

Sculpted Apostles

Kościół św Piotra i Pawła (Church of St Peter and St Paul; No 54) is a transcendent example of baroque architecture approached through a walled courtyard (originally the church graveyard) set with 12 late baroque sculptures of the apostles (1720s) by David Heel. The courtyard is a highly aesthetic overture to a magnificent baroque facade designed by Bernardoni of Como. Commissioned by the Jesuits, who came to Kraków in 1583, the design was modelled on two churches in Rome, San Andrea della Valle and Il Gesù, following the form of a Latin cross. Additional baroque elements were added by Zygmunt III Waza's architect Giovanni Batista Trevano. The impressive stucco work, at its finest in the apse, where it depicts scenes from the lives of St Peter and St Paul (1619–33), is by Giovanni Falconi.

Above: pharmacy on a corner of the historic ul Grodzka
Right: sculptures of the apostles outside the Church of St Peter and St Paul

The tomb of Fr Piotr Skarga (1536–1612), Poland's most renowned preacher, can be seen in the crypt. People still leave pleas for his intercession by his tomb. Fr Piotr was instrumental in gaining the support of Zygmunt III Waza in building the church; indeed the king put up most of the money.

An equally fine architectural paradigm is the neighbouring **Kościół św Andrzeja Apostoła** (Church of St Andrew the Apostle; No 56). An early Romanesque church with a pair of elegant towers, it was founded in 1086 by Duke Władysław Herman and withstood the Tartar siege of 1241 thanks to 1.5-m (5-ft) thick walls. The exquisite baroque interiors are on a far smaller scale than the facade suggests. Wall paintings by Balthazar Fontana and 18th-century stucco work and are set between a vaulted ceiling decorated with putti and acanthus leaves, and a stunning 18th-century marble floor. The highly gilded baroque altar is matched by a gilded limewood pulpit in the form of a fishing boat with putti clinging to the soaring mast. Adjoining the church is the 14th-century Klasztor Klarysek (Order of St Claire), established in Kraków in 1245 at the behest of Duke Leszek Biały.

Street of the Canons

Opposite the church, a small square named after St Mary Magdalene features a statue of Fr Piotr Skarga (1536–1612), and leads to the enchanting and tranquil ul Kanoniczna ('Street of the Canons'). This street of ornate houses and palaces was named after the clergymen from Wawel Castle who lived here in the 15th and 16th centuries. No 1 has an impressive baroque portal. The **Cricoteca Museum** (ul Kanoniczna 5; tel: 421 69 75; open Mon–Fri 10am–2pm; admission fee) traces the rise of the avant-garde Cricoteca Theatre, and presents a good example of Gothic architecture. Contrast this with the Renaissance facade of Dom Pod Trzema Koronami (House under Three Crowns) at No 7, home to the Centre for the Documentation of the Art of Tadeusz Kantor.

Look hard above the plain renaissance portal of No 6 to see the dingy wall painting of the Madonna of Częchostowa. Number 9 is a late 14th-century mansion (refurbished in the 19th century), while No 18 is the seat of the John Paul II Institute.

Dom Dziekański (Deacon's House) at No 21 is a gem. Originally late 14th-century, it features a spectacular portal and an arcaded cloister added in the 16th

century by Italian architect Santi Gucci. The 14th-century house at ul Kanoniczna 25 was once that of the medieval chronicler Jan Długosz, and subsequently the studio of Stanisław Wyspianski's father, a sculptor.

The **Muzeum Archidiecezjalne** (Archdiocesan Museum; ul Kanoniczna 19–21; tel: 421 89 63; open Tues–Fri 10am–4pm, Sat–Sun 10am–3pm; admission fee) emphasises the street's ecclesiastical character. Housed in a historic building, the museum's collection includes sacral art – paintings, sculpture, illuminated manuscripts, stained-glass windows – from the 12th to the 18th centuries. The Gothic sculptures of the Madonna and Child, and also the altar pieces, are particularly impressive.

Between 1952 and 1967, when he was Bishop of Kraków, Pope John Paul II would use a room in the museum as a study. This room has been replicated with the inclusion of personal effects to make it all the more authentic.

Coffee Among the Literati

A perfect retreat for a coffee break or snack is **U Literatów** (Among the Literati) café at No 7. A cobbled courtyard garden provides al fresco tables, while *fin-de-siècle* town-house interiors include sofas and a grand piano. If you prefer tea to coffee, then Demmer's Tea House at No 21 offers an amazing choice of 130 types of tea.

Return to ul Grodzka, head in the direction of the Wawel and you'll find ul Stradomska, a busy, gritty street with the beautiful **Kościół Księży Misjonarzy** (Church of the Missionary Priests) at No 4. The Church of the Missionary Priests, established in France by St Vincent a Paulo in 1625, came to Kraków in 1682 to set up a seminary for priests at Wawel Castle. The present church was completed between 1719 and 1728 in a late baroque style. The facade was inspired by Bernini's San Andrea al Quirinale church in Rome.

The stylised interiors were based on Borromini's work in some of Rome's finest churches, such as the Chapel of the Three Kings in the Palazzo di Propaganda Fide and the Gesù and Maria Church. The impressive main altar, dating from 1762 and fashioned from black marble, features statues of St Peter and St Andrew. The Regency-style organ dates from 1745, while the altar dedicated to the founder of the order St Vincent a Paulo, is mid-18th century. The vivid 'technicolour' polychromy of assorted religious figures that adorns the vaulted ceiling was completed in 1864.

Above: the beautiful Church of the Missionary Priests on ul Stradomska

7. PLAC MATEJKI AND THE NORTH *(see map, p54)*

Explore the north of the city around Plac Matejki (Matejko Square), including historic buildings and attractions such as the Monument to the Battle of Grunwald, House Under the Globe and the Fine Art Academy, together with historic churches, St Florian's Church, St Vincent a Paolo's Church and Church of the Nuns of the Visitation.

Leave the historic centre along ul Floriańska, proceed through Florian's Gate and continue past the Barbican to find the extensive Plac Matejki

The central feature of Plac Matejki, which is a showpiece of late 19th- and early 20th-century styles is **Pomnik Grunwaldzki** (Monument to the Battle of Grunwald). This commemorates one of the greatest battles in medieval Europe, fought in 1410 by almost 80,000 soldiers. Victory for the Polish and Lithuanian army over the Teutonic knights, effectively ended the knights' dominance in Poland. Sculpted by Antoni Wiwulski, the monument features an equestrian statue of King Władysław Jagiełło, with Lithuania's Duke Witold standing below, and the vanquished Grand Master of the Teutonic Knights lying beneath them. On either side of the monument victorious Polish knights collect Teutonic flags. The monument, commissioned by the renowned concert pianist and statesman Ignacy Paderewski was ceremonially unveiled on the 500th anniversary of the battle in 1910.

The square's architecture is eclectic. At No 13 the **Akademia Sztuk Pięknych** (Academy of Fine Arts) has a facade designed in 1879 by Maciej Moraczewski featuring a bust of Poland's finest painter, Jan Matejko, above the main entrance. Matejko, who was instrumental in establishing the academy before being appointed its first rector, had a studio here. His pupils included Józef Mehoffer and other members of the *Młoda Polska* movement.

St Florian's Remains

Kościół św Floriana (St Florian's Church, ul Warszawska 1) was built to house the remains of St Florian, which were brought to Poland in 1184 at the instigation of King Kazimierz Sprawiedliwy (Casimir the Righteous). St Florian, who became one of Kraków's patron saints, is shown in a 1686 painting by Jan Triciusz, the court painter of King Jan III Sobieski, near the main altar. Cartouches also depict scenes from the life of St Florian.

Consecrated in 1212, the church was originally built in a Romanesque style that was lost in refurbishments. Extensive early 20th-century restorations yielded the current blend of Gothic, Italianate baroque and rococo. Admire a 15th-century bas-relief of the Virgin Mary and a 1767 chapel dedicated to St Jan Kanty. Opposite St Florian's church, leading to Jalu Kurka Park, is the Sióstr Miłosierdzia (Sisters of Divine Mercy) convent at ul Warszawska, 13.

The **Kościół Księża Misjonarzy św Wincentego a Paulo** (Church of the Missionary Priests of St Vincent a Paolo; ul św Filipa 19) is a centre for the cult of Our

Right: Monument to the Battle of Grunwald

Lady of Lourdes. Built in 1876–7, it adjoins the 1863 missionaries' house dedicated to St Vincent a Paolo. As the congregation outgrew the church, it was extended (in 1911–12) to include a chapel with an emotive figure of Our Lady of Lourdes. This statue, which was brought to Kraków in 1866, and a painting of the Crucifixion are both said to have miraculous powers. The painting, brought here in 1976 from a church in Milatyn, near Lvov in the Ukraine, originated in Rome.

Aquiline Gargoyles

Continue past the brick stalls of Rynek Kleparski (Kleparz Market), turn right into ul Basztowa and you'll find the 1906 **Dom Pod Globusem** (House Under the Globe) at the junction with ul Długa. This, a geometric and uniform example of Secessionism, has none of the sense of colour and flamboyance evident in the city's other buildings of this period. Designed, and still used, as commercial premises, the building has a distinctive spire, with gargoyles in the form of eagles, topped by a globe. The interior murals are by the premier Secessionist painter, Mehoffer.

Continue along ul Basztowa, turn right into ul Krowoderska and you'll find **Kościół Wizytek** (Church of the Nuns of the Visitation) at No 16. The church is under the patronage of St Francis Salesian, whose mission was to provide religious education for the young. Designed by Giovanni Solari and the Jesuit priest and architect Stanisław Solski, it was consecrated in

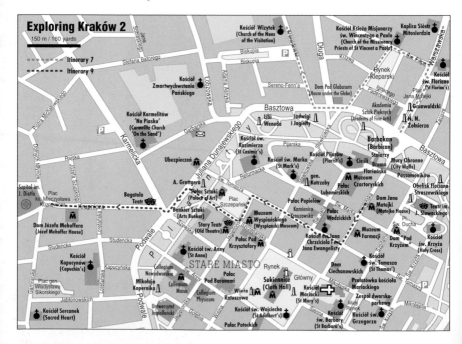

1695. This exquisite baroque building has a magnificent facade featuring an abundance of statuary. The stylised interiors include more statuary, especially by the main altar, beautiful side chapels, magnificent 17th-century polychromy designed by Jan Tryciusz and ornate stucco work. A painting of Matki Boskiej Nieustającej Pomocy (Our Lady of Eternal Intercession) that came from Rome is said to have miraculous powers. The Nuns of the Visitation convent, built around an attractive garden, adjoins the church.

8. THE CHURCHES OF EASTERN KRAKOW
(see map, p56)

This itinerary explores ul Kopernika's churches – St Nicholas' Church, Jesuits Church, Church of the Immaculate Conception of the BVM – as well as the Astronomical Observatory and Botanical Gardens.

You can see a fascinating range of historic churches just by strolling along ul Mikołaja Kopernika (Nicholas Copernicus Street). These include one of the city's oldest, **Kościół św Mikołaja** (St Nicholas' Church) at No 9. The earliest reference to this church dates from the 12th century, before it was rebuilt in a Romanesque style in 1229. In 1467 it was taken over by the Benedictine order – which had been established at the Abbey of Tyniec just outside Kraków since the 11th century – and 62 years later it was awarded collegiate status. For all the Gothic restyling of the 15th century, and the addition of baroque elements between 1677 and 1684, a fair number of original Romanesque sections have survived. Admire the main altar, which features a painting of St Nicholas, and also the baptismal font and a pentaptych of the Coronation of the Blessed Virgin Mary, which are both Gothic. The courtyard's medieval sculpture, known as the 'Lamp of the Dead', resembles a miniature church tower.

Cult of the Sacred Heart
Bazylika Najświętszego Serca Jezusowego, Jezuitów (Basilica of the Sacred Heart of Jesus, and Jesuit monastery) at No 26 is an extraordinary example of *fin-de-siècle* modernism, not just in terms of style, but also in scale – it's 52m (170ft) long, 19m (62ft) wide and has a 68-m (220-ft) high tower. First established in 1868, it evolved from a much smaller chapel attached to a Jesuit college for novices. In 1893 the Jesuits decided to turn the chapel into a church that would be Poland's centre of the cult of the Sacred Heart. It was designed by the celebrated architect Franciszek Mączyński and completed in 1920.

A number of the country's finest living artists and craftsmen were commissioned to work on the church. Note the entrance portal and integral sculptures by Ksawery Dunikowski. Particularly dazzling are Brother Wojciech Pieczowka's series of mosaics, including the magnificent

Above Left: St Florian's Church
Right: nuns near St Nicholas' church

Hold Narodu Polskiego Serca Bożemu (Homage of the Polish Nation to the Sacred Heart). Amazingly vivid Secessionist murals with floral motifs by Jan Bukowski extend along a nave that's remarkable for its granite and marble pillars. The neo-Renaissance main altar, with a colonnade supporting statuary, and a mosaic extending along the apse, is highly unusual and deeply emotive. A more recent addition is The Chapel of the Eternal Adoration of the Blessed Sacrament, completed in 1960, when the church was classified as a basilica. Since 1966 the basilica has been listed as a historic monument.

The mid 17th century baroque **Kosciół Niepokolanego Poczęcia NMP i św Łazarza** (Church of the Immaculate Conception of the Blessed Virgin Mary and St Valentine) at No 19 is set behind a walled forecourt. This church's most fascinating feature is a remarkable vaulted ceiling, painted a vivid blue. Since the 18th century, this has been the official church of the city's main hospital; numerous hospital buildings line both sides of the road.

Botanical Garden

Moving on from the ecclesiastical to the scientific, you'll find, at No 27, the **Observatorium Astronomiczne** (Astronomical Observatory). This palatial planetarium – part of the Jagiellonian University – is set in a late 18th-century neoclassical building. It adjoins the **Ogród Botaniczny** (Botanical Garden; open daily Apr–Oct, 9am–7pm; palm houses Sat–Thur 10am–6pm; Sun in winter 10am–2pm; tel: 663 3635; admission fee), which, established in 1783, is Poland's oldest such reserve. Originally comprising a mere 2.5ha (6 acres), it was laid out as an English-style landscaped park in 1820. Some of the trees planted then can be seen in the arboretum. The gardens were extended to their current size of almost 10ha (25 acres) after World War II. An extensive planting programme in the 1960s added lots of tropical specimens, and extra greenhouses in which to keep them.

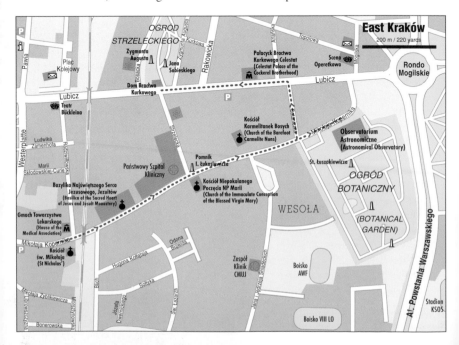

Like the observatory, the Garden is an adjunct of the university, and it has always emphasized its educational aspect. Any number of botanists have learned about their subject here, and the grounds are punctuated by statues of the country's leading figures in the field. In addition to the arboretum, there are medicinal shrubs, alpine plants (including specimens from the Carpathian Mountains, the Balkans, the Caucasus and the Alps), ponds, pools and lawns with ornamental borders. Two palm houses feature tropical and sub-tropical plants.

A small museum (open Apr–Oct Wed, Fri 10am–2pm, Sat 11am–3pm) housed in an attractive *fin-de-siècle* villa comprises a couple of galleries, though most exhibits are labelled only in Polish. Among the exhibits are assorted plant specimens and old prints and maps that outline the Garden's origins and evolution. One of the most interesting exhibits is a display cabinet inlaid with 260 types of wood, culled from trees native to or cultivated in Poland.

Cockerel Brotherhood

A short detour from ul Kopernika leads to **Muzeum Celestat** (Celestat Museum; ul Lubicz 16; tel: 429 3791; open Tues, Wed, Fri, Sat 9am–4pm, Thur 11am–6pm; admission fee except on Sat). This unusual museum recounts the history of an organisation that has been an integral element of the city for centuries. Still extant, the Bractwo Kurkowe (literally 'Cockerel Brotherhood') was established in medieval times to teach Kraków's civilians how to wield a rifle, should they be needed to defend the city.

The museum's collection includes portraits of champion marksmen and of course the club's mascot, the Silver Cockerel, which is a magnificent example of Renaissance art. The brotherhood's Corpus Christi procession, with participants dressed in historic uniforms, is an annual highlight in the old town. Three weeks later, in a traditional ceremony on the Main Market Square, the outgoing king of the brotherhood ceremonially presents the Silver Cockerel to the new incumbent. A short distance from the museum the Ogród Strzeleckiego ('Rifle Marksmens' Garden') is home to monuments to two Polish kings: Jan III Sobieski (1675–96) and Zygmunt August (1548–73).

Above: in the Basilica of the Sacred Heart of Jesus
Right: the basilica's 1920's exterior

9. MUSEUMS AND GALLERIES *(see map, p54)*

A look at some of Kraków's more specialised museums and galleries, including the preserved homes of Jan Matejko and Józef Mehoffer, modern art centres, the Pharmacy Museum and the Theatre Museum.

By any standards, Kraków is well-served by museums. These range from the vast National Museum to a series of fascinating mini-museums designed to document specific themes, historical eras and celebrated artists.

Dom Jana Matejki (Jan Matejko Museum; ul Floriańska 41; tel: 422 5926; open May–Oct Tues, Wed, Sat 10am–7pm, Thurs–Fri 10am–4pm, Sun 10am–3pm; Nov–Apr Wed–Thur, Sat–Sun 10am–3.30pm, Fri 10am–6pm; admission fee) was established in 1896 and is Poland's oldest biographical museum. Generally considered the greatest artist in the country's history, Matejko (1838–93) spent most of his life in this house, which comprehen-

sively details his body of work, including portraits, sculpture and his designs for the polychromy, stained-glass windows and altarpieces of some of Kraków's finest churches. Matejko's oeuvre has a resonance that goes far beyond his considerable influence on his contemporaries. At a time when Poland was partitioned and therefore didn't officially exist, his works were exhibited throughout Europe, and thus became an important symbol of Polish identity.

The museum has preserved the atmosphere of a private home, with the earliest sections dating from the 15th century. The grand first-floor salon overlooking ul Floriańska is furnished exactly as it was when Matejko lived here. There's neo-Renaissance furniture commissioned by the artist in Venice in 1878, a cabinet displaying some of his many awards and, in his bedroom, a beautifully painted skyscape ceiling. Self-portraits illustrate the young Matejko; a terracotta bust depicts him as an elderly maestro. The portrait gallery features pictures of Copernicus and King Jan III Sobieski's historic victory at the Battle of Vienna. Two galleries overlooking the inner courtyard show Matejko's designs for polychromy in St Mary's Church on the Main Market Square.

Matejko's Mementoes

Matejko's keen eye for period detail isn't limited to his own creations; it's also reflected in his collection of antique military and architectural pieces, a number of which can be found in the museum. Climb the stairs to the studio on the top floor, where you can see a wooden horse complete with a ceremonial saddle on which subjects could pose, and other mementoes such as Matejko's palette, spectacles, chess set and walking stick. Matejko's work can also be seen in the Gallery of 19th-Century Polish Painting and Sculpture in the Cloth Hall, and at the National Museum.

For a thorough account of the history of the pharmacy, pay a visit to

Above: street art. **Above Right:** stained-glass exhibit at the Museum of Pharmacy
Right: a reconstructed historic chemist's shop at the Museum of Pharmacy

Muzeum Farmacji (Museum of Pharmacy; ul Floriańska 25; tel: 421 9279; open Tues 3pm–7pm, Wed–Sun 11am–2pm; admission fee). The museum occupies an elegant town house with a Renaissance portal, as well as Gothic and baroque elements, and doesn't limit itself to its ostensible subject; it also covers interiors and decorative arts. The highlights of the various galleries are the replicated interiors of pharmacies throughout history. Also be sure to check out a fascinating collection of assorted urns, jars and other pharmaceutical accessories.

In the museum's cellars you will find antique distillation equipment and wine barrels. There was a time when, in the belief that alcohol promoted longevity and youthfulness, Polish apothecaries sold Italian and Hungarian wines – and, this being Poland, vodka – for medicinal purposes. Red wine was thought to be particularly beneficial.

The beautiful 19th-century stained-glass window on the first floor landing that pictures a pestle, mortar and various herbs, was taken from a chemist's shop in the city. The portrait gallery depicts various renowned apothecaries, while the reconstructed interiors show how pharmacies were furnished in various architectural styles. These include superb 19th-century neo-baroque and Biedermier examples. A stunning collection of porcelain and glass urns, used to store various ingredients, are complemented by calligraphically hand-written prescriptions. Exhibits of related items feature a collection of stamps from around the world that have pharmaceutical themes.

The city's chemist shops themselves also have some surprising features. There's a wonderful mosaic of a lion at Pod Złotym Lwem (Under the Golden Lion) pharmacy at ul Długa 4, and an impressive bas-relief at the Pod Złotym Tygrysem (Under the Golden Lion) pharmacy at ul Szczepańska 1. Pod Złotym Słoniem (Under the Golden Elephant) at Pl Wszystkich Swiętych 11 has retained the building's late 19th-century interiors.

Pl Szczepański (Szczepański Square) was named after the baroque Kościół

św Szczepana (Church of St Stephen). Built by the Jesuits in the 13th century, the church had been refurbished in a baroque style by the time it was demolished at the end of the 18th century. The square then became a marketplace, and is now a car park. Nevertheless, the surrounding buildings include a few interesting sights.

A 17th-century mansion with 19th-century additions provides a distinguished setting for the **Muzeum Stanisława Wyspiańskiego** (Stanisław Wyspiański Museum; ul Szcze-pańska 11; tel: 422 7021; open May–Oct Wed, Sat 10am–7pm, Thur–Fri 10am–4pm, Sun 10am–3pm; Nov–Apr Tues–Thur, Sat–Sun 10am–3.30pm, Fri 10am–6pm; admission fee). This was originally the residence of the Szołayski family, who donated the building to the National Museum in 1904. The collection covers the work of Wyspiański (1869–1907), one of Poland's foremost artists, poets and playwrights, and a leading member of the Młoda Polska (Young Poland) modernist movement. The museum inclues portraits, landscapes, designs for stage sets and architectural features that appeared in the city's buildings, such as stained-glass windows, which can be seen at the Basilica of St Francis of Assisi. There is also a collection of memorabilia, and graphic designs for various editions of his plays.

The Oldest Theatre

On the corner of the square, at the junction with ul Jagiellońska, you'll come across the **Stary Teatr** (Old Theatre; ul Jagiellońska 1). This, the city's oldest public theatre, was established in 1799 by the renowned actor Mateusz Witkowski. In its mid-19th century heyday, Helena Modrzejewska starred here in various roles before treading the boards in Warsaw and then the USA. The theatre closed in 1893, in the face of competition from the new

Słowacki Theatre, and it didn't re-open until 1945. It was refashioned with wonderful Secessionist details in 1903 by the architects Franciszek Mączyński and Tadeusz Stryjeński, both members of the *Młoda Polska* movement. The theatre now houses the **Stary Teatr Muzeum** (Museum of the Old Theatre; tel: 422 85 66; open Tues–Fri 11am–1pm, and also one hour before and during performances; admission fee), which traces the history of the building, various productions and the stars who performed here. If you're ready for a break, there is a neo-Secessionist café in the basement. Needless to say, the lugubrious café, all organic forms and undulating ceiling, attracts the thespian brigade.

You can see another good example of Secessionism in the apartment building at No 2, which dates back to 1909. A fine metalwork wreath crowns a stained-glass panel, with decorative balconies overlooking the square.

The Aesthetic Option

Two neighbouring buildings hold exhibitions of modern and contemporary art within very different settings. The aesthetic option is **Pałac Sztuki** (Palace of Art; Pl Szczepański 4; tel: 422 66 16; open daily 8.15am–6pm; admission fee), a Secessionist building designed by Franciszek Mączyński, with a highly decorative frieze by Jacek Malczewski that includes busts of Matejko and Wyspiański. The aptly named **Bunkier Sztuki** (Arts Bunker; Pl Szczepański 3a; tel: 421 38 40; open Tues–Sun 11am–6pm, Thur till 8pm; admission fee) is virtually the only intrusion of ugly, modern architecture in the city's historic centre. It holds interesting exhibitions of contemporary art.

Continue across the Planty Gardens, turn left to ul Podwale and then proceed along ul Krupnicza to reach **Dom Józefa Mehoffera** (Józef Mehoffer House; ul Krupnicza 26; tel: 421 11 43; open May–Oct Tues, Wed, Sat 10am–7pm, Thurs–Fri 10am–4pm, Sun 10am–3pm; Nov–Apr Wed–Thur, Sat–Sun 10am–3.30pm, Fri 10am–6pm; admission fee). One of Poland's finest painters, Mehoffer (1869–1946) was a pupil of Matejko and, together with Wyspiański, a pioneer of modernism. In addition to landscapes, portraits and still life, he designed stained-glass windows and polychromy.

Most of the house is furnished as it was in the artist's day. It's as interesting for its stylish period interiors as for the abundance of Mehoffer's works. The elegant dining room features charcoal portraits and architectural drawings of Kraków such as the Market Square in 1903. In the library hangs a 1943 painting of the garden (which can be visited April–Oct). The salon has a collection of family portraits and there are two vast designs for stained-glass windows over the staircase. Secessionist furnishings include linen curtains embroidered with butterflies in Mehoffer's bedroom. By contrast, a Japanese room with scarlet walls and lacquered cabinets is a treasure trove of Oriental *objets d'art*.

Above Left: bust of Matejko, Palace of Art. **Left:** lovers unite in central Kraków
Above: Józef Mehoffer House pays tribute to the Secessionist artist

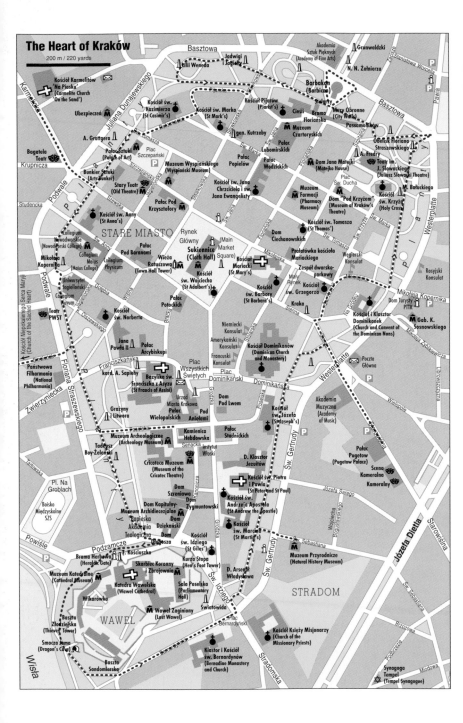

The Heart of Kraków

200 m / 220 yards

10. GREEN KRAKOW (see map, p82)

This itinerary explores the 'green' route around the historic centre.

Start by the subway leading to the railway station

The starting point is a good place in which to pick up a snack, typically, from a stall tended by a friendly 'granny'. Recommended street food includes *obwarzanki* (bread rings flavoured with either rock salt or poppy seeds) and *świderki* (literally 'little drills' – sweet, brioche-style bread fingers). For extra sustenance, try a *brinza* (smoked ewe's-milk cheese produced by Highlanders). Emerging from the subway, you'll see on the left Obelisk Floriana Straszewskiego, a monument that honours a mid-19th century senator who was instrumental in planning the layout of the Planty Gardens.

The **Planty Gardens** form a green horseshoe around the city centre. Take a round-trip walk of some 3.5km (2 miles) and you'll find plenty of benches on which to rest, and numerous side streets to explore. The Planty Gardens, actually a series of individual gardens, are short on flowers but big on shaded avenues, lawns, water features and monuments. The gardens were created in the 1820s when the Austrian authorities decided to demolish the medieval city walls. Throughout the Planty foundations of the original walls can still be seen, and plaques indicate the sites where bastions once stood.

Victims of Communist Aggression

Continue in the direction of the Barbican and you will pass a far smaller monument dedicated to **Ofiarom Komunistycznej Prowokacji** (Victims of Communist Aggression). Unveiled in 1936, this depicts trade union members clashing with the police. The flamboyant late 19th-century **Teatr im J Słowackiego** (Juliusz Słowacki Theatre) on the left, one of the city's leading theatrical venues, was modelled on the Paris Opera House.

Above: the Planty Gardens feature lots of tranquil shaded avenues
Right: looking forward to a bright future

Pass Florian's Gate on the left and you'll arrive at the **Barbakan** (Barbican; open daily 10.30am–6pm; admission fee). Recently reopened after a 10-year restoration programme, the Barbican is one of Europe's biggest and best-preserved examples of medieval defensive architecture. King Jan Olbracht laid the foundation stone of this circular Gothic building that has walls up to 3.5m (11ft) wide at the base. It was surrounded by a deep moat more than 25m (82ft) wide, and linked to Florian's Gate by '*szyja*' ('the neck') – basically a bridge leading over another moat. Walk around the battlements for fine views across the Planty and the integral courtyard.

Monument To A Muse

Adjoining the final section of the city walls is the rear of the **Arsenał Miejski** (City Arsenal), now part of the Czartoryski Museum. After the arsenal you'll see one of the largest of the Planty's water features, where silver birch trees, ponds and a fountain create an atmospheric setting for the 1886 statue of the poet Bohdan Zalewski. Another 1886 monument, by Oskar Sosnowski, marks the quincentenary of the Polish-Lithuanian Commonwealth, and depicts Queen Jadwiga and Duke Władysław Jagiełło. Opposite the junction of ul Pijarska and ul św Marka is Daun's statue of his muse, Lilla Weneda.

Proceed along ul Pijarska, with fragments of the original city walls to your left, turn into ul Reformacka and you'll find Kościół św Kazimierza (Church of St Kasimir), a 17th-century baroque affair with fine Secessionist polychromy. Cross ul św Tomasza to ul Szczepańska and the corner of Szczepański Square. On the left is the flamboyantly elegant, Secessionist **Pałac Sztuki** (Palace of Art); opposite is the 1960s Bunkier Sztuki (Arts Bunker). Both exhibit modern and contemporary art. On the right Wacław Szymanowski's attractive 1901 Secessionist monument to the renowned Kraków painter Artur Grottger is set in a semi-circular flowerbed. By the junction with ul Szewska, Kawiarnia u Zalipanek (Zalipanek Café) has an attractive open-air terrace with views of the Planty.

Of the buildings on ul Karmelicka, Kościół Karmelitow 'Na Piasku' (Carmelite church and convent 'On the Sands'; No 19) dates from the 11th century and features the 'miraculous' painting of Our Lady of the Sands. By ul Gołębia (Pigeon Street) you'll find a small wooded enclave with a

statue of Copernicus dating from 1900.

A Matejko portrait of Copernicus can be seen in the assembly hall of the adjacent Collegium Novum (ul Gołębia 24). This neo-Gothic building, designed by Feliks Księżarski and built in 1883–7, features crests of the Jagiellonian University in the facade. (It now serves as the university's administrative centre.) The Nazis arrested 184 academics here: they died in Sachenhausen concentration camp. The college counts King Jan III Sobieski and Pope John Paul II among its alumni.

Turn into ul Smolensk and find the 1884 Kościół Niopokalnego Serca Maryjl (Church of the Sacred Heart of the Blessed Virgin Mary) at No 6. This is where the pope prayed when he was Bishop of Kraków. Nuns from the adjoining Convent of St Felicity painted the Stations of the Cross and the mural of Our Lady by the main altar in the 1950s. After ul Franciszkanska and ul Poselska with the **Archaeology Museum** at No 3 (tel: 422 7100; open Mon–Wed 9am–2pm, Thur 2–6pm, Fri, Sun 10am-2pm; Jul–Aug same hours as before but Tues 2–6pm; admission fee) you pass a monument to the translator and arts critic Tadeusz Boy-Żelenski (1874–1941), before reaching Wawel Royal Castle. Turn left into Podzamcze and walk past Smocza Jama (Dragon's Cave) to ul Bernardynska, with the **Klasztor i Kościoł Bernardynów** (Bernardine Monastery and Church) at No 2. The Bernardine Order was established here in the 15th century, although this baroque church is 17th century. Later details include Mehoffer's stained-glass windows depicting the life of St Simon, a 15th-century Bernardine monk.

Our Lady of the Snow

Continue along the Planty, past the Royal Hotel, and into ul św Sebastiana with the Natural History Museum (Muzeum Przyrodnicze) at No 9 (Mon–Thur 9am–5pm, Fri–Sun 9am–6pm; admission fee) housed in the Secessionist-style former public baths. On ul Starowislna are the 19th-century Academy of Music (No 3) and Pugetów Palace (No 15). Overlooking the Planty, **Kościół i Klasztor Dominlkanek** (Church and Convent of the Dominican Nuns; ul Mikołajska 21) were founded by Duchess Anna Lubomirska in the 1630s. Observe the elegant baroque interiors, ornamental vaulted ceiling and early 20th-century neo-baroque main altar. The 17th-century painting of Matka Boska Śnieżna (Our Lady of the Snow), a gift from Pope Urban VIII, is said to have miraculous powers. When the Swedes invaded in the 17th century, Our Lady of the Snow appeared above the convent, shielding it from attack with Her cape. The astonished Swedes abandoned their siege and the convent survived.

A little further along you'll come to the Zakopianka café and restaurant, with *al fresco* tables overlooking the Planty. Nearby is the Florian Straszewski obelisk and the subway leading down to the railway station.

Left: the Julius Słowacki Theatre was modelled on the Paris Opera House
Above: the Barbican is one of Europe's finest examples of medieval ramparts

Excursions

1. ZAKOPANE *(see map, p68)*

A pretty holiday resort that's home to the ethnic Górals, a traditional retreat for intellectuals, and a winter skiing venue.

The train journey from the main station takes up to four hours; one of the frequent buses from the bus station will get you there in about two hours

The enchanting little town of Zakopane, one of Poland's most popular tourist resorts, is known for its beautiful mountain scenery in summer and prime skiing in winter. Set at the foot of the Tatra Mountains, Zakopane was, from around the 16th century, a Góral sheep-farming village. The Górals are a small ethnic group of highlanders from the Podhale and Pieniny regions, to which they are thought to have migrated from the north of Poland in the 13th century. They speak their own dialect and maintain traditional customs, including folk music and dancing. Zakopane's restaurants and concert halls often feature performances by Góral choirs and dance troupes. Vernacular architecture is characterised by wooden buildings adorned with carvings and painted rustic motifs – the churches are particularly beautiful.

A Symbol of Resistance

Poland 'discovered' Zakopane in the 1870s when a Warsaw doctor, Tytus Chałubiński, first visited what was then a village. The first hotel was built in 1885 to accommodate a specific clientele: artists and intellectuals inspired by the Górals' indomitable sense of independence. The Górals were seen as a symbol of resistance to occupations by Prussia, Russia and Austria.

Zakopane became a bohemian centre at the start of the 20th century, with a cultural guest list starring the likes of Nobel prize-winning novelist Henryk Sienkiewicz and concert pianist Ignacy Paderewski. Some of Poland's leading artists established permanent homes here, and elements of Góral culture began to appear in the work of composers such as Karol Szymanowski and writers like Jan Kasprowicz. The painter, architect and critic Stanisław Witkiewicz was a key figure in propagating the 'Zakopane style'.

A stroll along ul Kościeliska gives an idea of the town's architectural idiosyncrasies. In 1893 Witkiewicz based his **Villa Koliba** (ul Kościeliska 18; tel: 201 3602; open Wed–Sat 9am–4.30pm, Sun 9am–3pm; admission fee) on a highlander's cottage; the largest villa he designed, in 1908, is the Dom Pod Jedlami on ul Koziniec 1. This street is also the location

Left: Villa Koliba, based on a highlander's cottage
Right: stocking up on provisions at the market

of Zakopane's earliest church, the mid-19th century **Stary Kościół Farny** (Old Parish Church). In the cemetery you'll find the tombstones of several famous figures, including Witkiewicz and Chałubiński.

Ul Krupówki runs from the train station past the 1877–96 neo-Romanesque **Krupówki Kościół Parafialny** (Krupowki parish church). Witkiewicz designed its **Kaplica Jana Chrzciciela i Matki Bożej Różancowej** (Chapels of John the Baptist and Our Lady Mary of the Rosary), as well as the stained-glass windows and polychromy, in the Zakopane style. The **Muzeum Tatrzańskie** (Tatra Museum; ul Krupówki 10; tel: 201 5205; open Tues–Sat 9am–4.30pm, Sun 9am–3pm; admission fee) has a fine collection of folk art.

The Villa Atma's **Karol Szymanowski Museum** (ul Kasprusie 19; tel 201 3493; open Wed, Thur, Sat, Sun 10am–3.30, Fri 12–6pm; admission fee) was home to the composer in the 1930s. In Jaszczurowka, on Zakopane's outskirts, the beautiful **Kaplica Najświętszego Serca Pana Jezusa** (Chapel of the Most Sacred Heart of Jesus, 1908) was designed by Witkiewicz. Zakopane is still a thriving home to the arts, with renowned productions at the Teatr im S Ignacego Witkiewicza at ul Chramcówki 15. And every August, since 1962, locals and expat Górals enjoy the Festival of Highland Folklore.

Zakopane is known for summers that can last till October, and for its green spaces; some 12 percent of the land within the town limits is forest, and

Around Kraków

16 km / 10 miles

a vast meadow fills the heart of the town. The region is popular with hikers – numerous well-marked trails lead to the gorgeous alpine scenery of the Tatra Mountains. The largest of the area's many waterfalls and lakes, Morskie Oko (Eye of the Sea), can easily be reached by bus from Zakopane.

Zakopane draws three million visitors every year, especially in the skiing season (Nov–Apr) when excellent facilities cater for enthusiasts of all grades. The slopes are good, there are several jumps, and more than 50 ski lifts access the most popular mountain, Kasprowy (1,985m/6,510 ft). The tourist information centre is at ul Kościuszki 17 (tel: 201 2211; www.zakopane.pl).

2. AUSCHWITZ *(see map, p68)*

The Nazi death camp, now a UNESCO World Heritage site and museum.

Trains go from the main station to Oświęcim, where buses run to the camp

The town of Oświęcim (Auschwitz) will always be synonymous with the Holocaust. Now an industrial centre, situated south of Katowice, Poland's key industrial conurbation, Oswięcim, is around 65km (40 miles) from Kraków. The site of a castle in the 12th century, it became the capital of an independent dukedom in 1317 and part of Poland in 1457. In the years of Poland's partition (1772–1918) the town was part of Austria.

Shortly after they invaded Poland in 1939, the Nazis built the Auschwitz-Birkenau concentration camp. The largest such complex in the country, it comprised two camps covering an area of 172 hectares (425 acres). Auschwitz was a slave-labour camp largely reserved for political prisoners, members of the resistance and other 'opponents' of the Nazi regime – mainly Poles and Germans; Birkenau was an extermination camp. The entrance gate to the camp bears the notorious motto, *Arbeit Macht Frei* (Work Makes You Free).

Transported in cattle trucks from all over Europe, an estimated 1.5 million prisoners from 28 nations lost their lives here. Arrivals were divided into those capable of work and others, who were taken straight to the gas chambers. The vast majority of victims were Jews, there were numerous Polish, Russian and gypsy inmates too. Many died as a result of slave labour, hunger, illness and torture. The genocide peaked in 1942, when the gas chambers killed up to 20,000 people per day. Corpses were incinerated and buried in mass graves.

Liberated by the Red Army

Before retreating in 1944, the Nazis began destroying the evidence of their horrific crimes. They detonated the crematoria and some camp buildings, but did not have enough time to destroy the gas chambers. The camp was liberated by Russia's Red Army in 1945.

Auschwitz-Birkenau was established as a National Museum of Martyrology (open daily 8am–dusk; admission fee) in 1947, and in

Right: watchtower at the Museum of Martyrology

1979 it was listed by UNESCO as a World Heritage Site. To visit the camps you must join a guided tour; children under the age of 12 aren't admitted. Documentary film and photos from the Auschwitz archives include footage shot by the troops who liberated the camp. The museum illustrates the struggle and martyrdom of daily life at Auschwitz, with heartbreaking exhibits such as children's clothes and photographs of the victims. A monument to the Victims of Auschwitz stands in the grounds of the camp in Birkenau.

3. WIELICZKA SALT MINE *(see map, p68)*

A subterranean expedition to one of the continent's oldest working mines, which also features a museum, chapels and, on ground level, the historic Saltmaster's Castle.

Wieliczka can be reached by minibuses, which leave from ul Warszawska, or take a train from the main railway station

The town of Wieliczka, which received its charter in 1289, developed around the highly lucrative salt-mining trade. The salt was initially obtained from various springs that bubbled up in the area, a process so successful that, in the 14th and 15th centuries, this was one of the continent's most important mining towns. Today a feature on UNESCO's World Cultural Heritage List, **Kopalnia Soli Wieliczka** (Wieliczka Salt Mines; ul Daniłowicza; tel: 278 73 02; open daily Apr–Oct 7.30am–7.30pm; Nov–March 8am–5pm; by guided tour only (available in different languages), individual tourists must wait for a tour group to be assembled; admission fee) is Poland's and possibly the world's oldest working salt mine. Tickets, books and souvenirs can also be purchased in Kraków at ul Wiślna 12a (tel: 426 2050; www.kopalnia.pl).

Dating back to the 12th – or, according to some sources, the 10th – century, and located around 13km (7 miles) outside Kraków, the mine area now consists of a number of related attractions, with the museum alone comprising eight separate levels that reach a depth of 315m (1,000ft). The salt lodes are 1km wide and 6km (3½ miles) long and, measured together, the total,

labyrinthine length of all the mine's galleries, chambers and tunnels extends to more than 150km (nearly 100 miles).

A Million Visitors

Every year, Wieliczka receives almost a million visitors. It has a 2-km (1-mile) tourist trail that descends to level three – some 135m (44ft) underground – making for a moderately strenuous two-hour tour, the descent into the mine being by stairway (although lift access can be arranged). Tourists are frequently amazed by the museum, which gives a comprehensive overview of salt-mining through the centuries. Displayed in authentic surroundings, the exhibition incorporates

Left: in the Chapel of St Kinga

the world's largest collection of historic mining equipment, with an assortment of hoists and horse-drawn mechanisms featuring prominently.

The chambers' extraordinary natural attractions include caverns with saltwater lakes, and bas-reliefs and sculptures fashioned from rock salt. The mines have three chapels: one honouring St Anthony, one dedicated to St Barbara, the patron saint of miners and, most fascinating of all, the largest – the Chapel of St Kinga. The size of a small church, it is lit by chandeliers created from rock salt which, together with the carvings, sculptures and the main altar form an extraordinarily magical 'underworld'. You can even get married here. The tour culminates in a large chamber, with an express lift up to a viewing platform.

An Underground Sanatorium

If you have a fear of confined spaces, this is probably not an expedition for you. It's possible to leave the tour at only a few locations, and even if you do get out early, you may need to wait your turn for the cramped cage lift back up to ground level. Since the mid-19th century, when salt baths were first recognised for their potential as healing agents, Wieliczka has also enjoyed the benefits of a sanatorium. Today its underground chambers, which reach a depth of 211m (690ft), are still used as a location for the treatment of respiratory illnesses, particularly asthma, and allergies.

Another museum, on ground level, is the neighbouring **Zamek Żupny** (Saltmaster's Castle; open May–Sept Mon, Wed–Fri 10am–5pm; admission fee). Originally a 13th-century fortress that was turned into a Renaissance castle during the 16th century, this is the country's sole example of medieval architecture relating to salt mining and trading. To see an exhibition focusing on the ancient and early medieval history of Wieliczka, you have to go underground once more – it's in the original 13th- to 15th-century cellars. The 16th-century Gothic hall, with a vaulted ceiling supported by a single

Above: St Anthony's Chapel is one of three in the salt mine

pilaster, is hung with portraits of the castle's former salt lords. A remarkable collection of salt cellars – with highly decorative glass, silver and faïence examples – reflects various styles from the 18th to the 20th centuries. The display also features Polish and other European porcelain, and showcases the work of the genre's biggest names, such as Meissen. Other buildings within the castle complex include a 14th-century Gothic bastion and defensive walls, a warehouse, guardhouse and the kitchen where the miners ate their meals.

In addition to the salt mine and castle, this historic town has a traditional market square and two churches of note. **Kościół św Klemensa** (St Clement's Church) dates from the 14th century and is especially worth visiting for its baroque chapel. At the 16th-century **Kościół św Sebastiana** (St Sebastian's Church) you'll find Włodzimierz Tetmajer's wonderful early 20th-century polychromy of sacral and Gothic motif. Those interested in neoclassical architecture will appreciate the 18th-century **Knopków Palace** and, from the 19th century, the **Turówka salt warehouse**.

4. PIESKOWA SKALA CASTLE *(see map, p68)*

Surrounded by stunning scenery, this beautiful castle is now a museum with exhibits dating back to the Middle Ages.

Buses depart from Kraków's main bus station

Around 30km (20 miles) northwest of Kraków, the **Castle of Pieskowa Skała** lies within the Krakowsko-Częstochowska Jura mountain range. This dramatic terrain features limestone hills and cliffs, caves, deep valleys and weird-shaped rocks that resemble clubs and needles. One such rock just a short walk from the castle is the 25-m (82-ft) high Club of Hercules. Pieskowa Skała ('Dog's Rock') was originally one of several hilltop castles built on the so-called Trail of the Eagle's Lair that defended the route from Kraków to Silesia during the Middle Ages. The castle overlooks the Prądnik Valley and, whatever your perspective, the views are magnificent.

Built in the Gothic style by King Kazimierz Wielki (Kasimir the Great),

the castle was acquired by the Szafraniec family and adapted into a private residence at the end of the 14th century. Renaissance elements were added during the mid-16th century refurbishment modelled on Kraków's Wawel Castle and the similarities between the two, particularly the stunning arcaded courtyard (though Pieskowa Skała's is on a far smaller scale) are striking.

The castle was subsequently owned by two other aristocratic families until the beginning of the 19th century, when it declined into a ruin. Restored and converted into a hotel, but maintaining the Gothic and Renaissance elements that make it one of the most beautiful castles in Poland, it became a museum after World War II. Today the museum is a branch of Wawel Castle's National Art Collection (Sułoszowa 4; tel: 389 60 04; open Tues–Fri 10am–3.30pm, Sat, Sun 10am–5.20pm; admission fee). Exhibits include paintings and furniture from the Middle Ages to the 19th century. The ground floor of the palace houses the Zamkowa restaurant.

Above: Pieskowa Skała Castle is within a protected national park
Right: built on a limestone cliff, Tyniec Abbey overlooks the Vistula River

5. TYNIEC ABBEY *(see map, p68)*

A Benedictine monastery and fortress that's nearly 1,000 years old, Tyniec is now a fascinating reminder of successive waves of invasion.

Tyniec can be reached by bus from Kraków's main bus station

The **Benedictine Abbey** (tel: 567 59 77; open daily 6am–6.30pm) in Tyniec, about 10km (6 miles) west of Kraków, enjoys a romantic location at the summit of a 40-m (130-ft) high limestone cliff overlooking the Vistula River and a swathe of pastoral landscapes. The abbey was founded by King Kazimierz Odnowiciel (Casimir the Restorer), who originally built it as a Romanesque abbey-fortress designed to be part of Kraków's town fortifications. The king invited the Benedictine order to settle in Tyniec in 1044, and before long the monks – whose motto: *'ora et labora'* means 'prayer and work' – were educating young Polish noblemen at the abbey.

The church and monastery's architecture spans various styles, following repeated acts of destruction – by the Tartars in 1242, the Swedes in 1672 and the Russians in 1771. Only fragments of the original Romanesque **Kościół św Piotra i Pawła** (Church of St Peter and St Paul) have survived. The church was given a Gothic makeover in the 15th century and a baroque facelift in the 17th century, when the cloisters were added.

Organ Recitals

The monastery's Renaissance style dates from the 1560s. The abbey's impressive gateways are a reminder of its original defensive role, while one of the courtyards features a well, dating from the 1620s, with an octagonal slate roof, like a small pagoda, which was constructed without any nails. Although parts of the abbey are still undergoing restoration work, it hosts the Days of Organ Music and Tyniec Organ Recitals festivals in July and August.

The area around Tyniec is well worth exploring. The local inhabitants have preserved their characteristic folklore, the *folklor krakówski* – especially the traditional national costumes, the music and a wonderful dance known as the *krakówiak* – and the surrounding villages comprise a treasure chest of architecture particular to this region. Today's builders frequently retain the methods and tools favoured by their forebears.

Leisure Activities

SHOPPING

Just like the city's historic attractions, a large proportion of Kraków's finest shopping opportunities are conveniently located in the centre. Although the shops may seem small and old-fashioned when compared with their counterparts in major Western European cities, and despite there being only one department store in the centre, there is nevertheless plenty on offer. You should be able to find a decent choice of fashion, leather goods and accessories, tableware, glassware, and of course souvenirs.

Amber

Amber is the country's national stone, and jewellery made from either amber or silver, or often both, often represents exceptionally good value, whether it is in the form of rings, earrings, necklaces, bracelets, cufflinks, or even lampshades and jewellery boxes. The colour of this luminous, transparent stone ranges across a surprising spectrum of hues, from yellow and white to stones with red and green streaks and tinges. Don't consider these tints as flaws, but rather think of them as adding character.

Amber is actually fossilised resin that once seeped from deciduous and coniferous trees, solidified and, over the course of thousands of years, matured into the form we are familiar with today. This resin would sometimes trap insects and flora, and amber that contains identifiable specimens of prehistoric life is considered a special rarity, and priced accordingly. The sea washes amber up from beneath the surface of the sand, depositing it conveniently on beaches to be collected by people.

Antiques

Although there are quite a number of interesting antiques shops in the city centre, you can't actually purchase anything in them. It is illegal to export items produced before 1945 – unless you succeed in eliciting written permission from the appropriate government department beforehand. (If you are tempted to break the law, be warned that border guards slap a harsh fine on anyone caught attempting to export antiques illegally – and they will also confiscate the items in question.)

Shopping areas

The principal shopping thoroughfares in the city centre are ul Floriańska, the Main Market Square, and ul Grodzka, which link up conveniently to form a 'shopping itinerary'. It's worth shopping at any number of the stores in these streets, but it can be difficult to recommend specific outlets and locations for two reasons. It's not uncommon for shops here to have no street number, which can confuse Western consumers. And some stores, in keeping with the legacy of the communist era, display only generic titles such as 'Jeweller', and don't seem to have a proprietary name. Marketing methods in Poland still have a long way to go before they reach Western levels.

Left: amber is Poland's national stone
Right: antiques are not for export

Imported goods can often be as expensive as they are in their country of origin, so you shouldn't expect to buy international brand names at a knock-down rate. Polish goods are considerably cheaper, and an increasing range of the country's brand names offer quality as well as classic or innovative design. Many shops accept credit cards, and typical opening hours are Mon–Fri 11am–7pm, Sat 10am–2 or 3pm.

The optimum place from which to embark on a shopping trip is on ul Floriańska by Florian's Gate. Elegant leather goods including handbags, gloves, coats, jackets and luggage are available at **Wittchen** (No 44), with shoes and boots next door at **Ecco** (No 42).

Continuing towards the Main Market Square, **Voight** at No 47 offers a handsome selection of international designer sunglasses; **Suknie Ślubne** (Wedding Dresses) at No 49 incorporates a range of wedding accessories, while **Jubiler** (Jeweller) at No 42 sells an elegant array of expensive jewellery. The exchange counter at No 37 usually offers some of the best rates. At No 31 is an attractive range of souvenirs, including folk art, ceramics, carvings and Christmas decorations.

Various fur and winter hats, sheepskin coats, jackets and accessories, together with a choice of Polish and international designer wear are available at **Furspol** (No 24). For smart, albeit traditional, men's and women's fashions try **Wiktorex** (No 32). If you're looking for younger men's designs, including shirts, coats, jackets, ties and accessories, go to the neighbouring **Reserved** (No 43). Whereas **Dziedziniec** (No 23) has an excellent choice of fur and sheepskin coats, hats and relevant accessories, **Oxa** (No 20) offers formal evening wear, cocktail dresses and modern sophisticated fashions by top European designers. Meanwhile, the neighbouring **Adidas** store carries that brand's famous array of sportswear.

A good choice of Polish vodkas and non-alcoholic drinks is available at No 23, with a handy grocery/deli also at No 51.

If you're in the market for top quality porcelain, crystal, tableware and glassware by leading European manufacturers – all elegantly displayed – **Belarte** (No 15) has the best line-up in town. At No 16 is a shop called **The Art of Polish Tableware**, with contemporary designs for the table, together with a selection of jewellery.

Sophisticated men's fashions are on offer at **Pabia** (No 7), in a smart, chandeliered setting, with jewellery and watches available from **W Kruk** (No 5), one of Poland's most traditional jewellers. You can get cosmetics from a local branch of **Helena Rubinstein** (No 1).

Turning left into the Main Market Square, **Elegance** (No 44) has the finest selection of quality shoes from foreign – including American and Italian – manufacturers. Footwear here ranges from casual, through

formal, to glitzy nightclub styles.

Continue to the corner with ul św Jana and you'll find the **Wedel** confectionery shop, from which you can buy various chocolates, gingerbread, cakes and other items to delight anyone with a sweet tooth. International brand-name watches, as well as jewellery (pearls, amber, silver and gold) are displayed at **IE In Jubiler** (No 39/40). At No 36 is **Księgarnia Muzyczna**, specialising in music, with publications and various CDs.

A good choice of casualwear is available from **Jackpot & Cottonfield** on the corner with Sławkowska. Students of German literature might be interested to see the plaque on the Jackpot & Cottonfield facade which states that Goethe stayed in this building on 5–7 September 1790.

Continue along the Main Market Square to the junction with ul Wiślna and ul św Anny to find the centre's single department store, **Galeria Centrum**. A well decorated emporium, it covers the expected range of cosmetics, perfumes, men's and women's fashion, shoes, leather goods and luggage. It has a gift wrapping service and, specially for foreign visitors, a currency exchange counter. Its opening hours are longer than the norm: Mon–Fri 9.30am–8.30pm, Sat 8am–8pm, Sun 10am–5pm.

Continuing around the Main Market Square leads to **Empik** (No 5), which sells cameras and films, and which will develop your film for you. Empik also has the city centre's best selection of foreign-language newspapers and magazines as well as CDs and DVDs.

At the centre of the Main Market Square, the **Cloth Hall** occupies a historic shopping venue. The range of goods on offer at this market of wooden stalls includes superior souvenirs, folk arts and crafts (such as the traditional nativity cribs and regional costumes that are so popular in these parts), leather goods and jewellery. The Cloth Hall's arcades also provide gallery space for amateur artists. Flea markets are sometimes held in the market square.

Heading in the direction of the adjacent ul Grodzka, the short stretch that leads to Plac Dominikanski has several up-market boutiques. **Paradise** (No 5) stocks men's

and women's designer finery; neighbours such as **Lacoste** and **Marlboro Classics** ofer more fashion.

When crossing Plac Dominkański, you might want to take a short detour to **Janina** (Plac Dominkański 5). This specialist store might look like a miniature doll's house, but it stocks more than 800 ties and bow ties. Next door is Demmer's Tea House, with a vast selection of speciality teas.

Continuing along ul Grodzka, **Shiva** (Nos 23 and 28) comprises two neighbouring shops specialising in Indian products such as clothes, textiles, tableware, carved animals and all sorts of musical instruments.

At No 29 **Amber** carries plenty of jewellery sporting the stone after which it's named. Neighbours include the **Levis** store, and the **Jan Feykel Gallery**, which deals in contemporary art.

As you stroll along ul Grodzka in the direction of Wawel Castle, you'll find more specialist stores. These include **Galeria Autorska Marianna Gołogórskiego Polskie Szkło** (No 58), whose wide range of Polish glassware includes stained-glass panels and paperweights; **Conrad Remani** for up-market leather and fur jackets and accessories; and its neighbour, **De Mehlem**, which sells similarly up-market leather handbags, elegant accessories and luggage.

Left: the Cloth Hall's arcades showcase the works of amateur artists
Above: open-air art gallery by St Florian's Gate

EATING OUT

Herrings and stuffed cabbage leaves are typical of the clichéd dishes that represent Polish cuisine in the minds of the uninitiated. In reality, the country's food tends to be light and elegant, and is prepared from specialities such as Baltic salmon, truffles and various types of mushroom. On the heavier side, game dishes (particularly venison and wild boar) are popular. Typical garnishes are prepared from soured cream, parsley or dill, which is the national herb.

A broad repertoire of soups includes *barszcz* (beetroot soup) which, when served cold with soured cream during the summer, is known as *chłodnik*. You might also try wild mushroom soup or *żur* (fermented rye soup served with sausage and potato).

Zrazy, which consists of seasoned sirloin of beef beaten and rolled around a filling of chopped fried bacon, breadcrumbs, dill cucumber and mushrooms, originated in Kraków. *Zrazy* are usually accompanied by another Kraków classic, buckwheat, and a cucumber salad known as *mizeria* ('misery'), which dresses the ingredients in condiments. *Mizeria* consists of wafer-thin slices of cucumber dressed in a combination of soured cream, lemon juice, a dash of caster sugar and salt, and garnished with minced dill or spring onion. This salad is attributed to the Italian princess Bona Sforza, who married King Zygmunt Stary at the beginning of the 16th century. According to some, the salad's cheerless name derives from the princess's propensity for weeping nostalgically for Italy whenever she ate it (though this version of the myth does claim that she enjoyed a happy-ever-after, fairy-tale existence). Alternatively, Bona Sforza may have eaten *mizeria* in such enormous quantities that the consequent pain of indigestion made her ask for a misericord (a dagger for committing suicide).

As a result of the Austro-Hungarian legacy, dishes such as goulash and *Viener Schnitzel* (pork escalope fried in breadcrumbs) are staples in the city's restaurants. The taste for cakes is another example of Austria's influence. Among the most popular cakes are *sernik* (cheesecake), which is prepared with either curd or cream cheese and always baked, and *makowiec* (poppy seed cake), which is prepared like a Swiss roll, around a creamy filling flavoured with poppyseeds.

The post-communist restaurant scene in Kraków is vibrant and diverse – you'll find many of the world's cooking traditions here. And, with so many restaurants located in historic buildings, there is no shortage of vaulted cellars in which to dine. Poland's gastronomic scene has evolved with amazing speed since the dark days of communism, when rationing and frequent shortages amounted to the virtual disappearance of

Above: Main Market Square has a number of discreet, elegant restaurants

Polish cuisine. Chefs had to follow state cookery manuals, and changes in restaurant menus, either seasonal or annual, were forbidden. Only since privatisation in 1989 have chefs been able to develop their own ideas, and rely on regular supplies.

Encouraged by the revival of real Polish food, chefs began to reinterpret national dishes: the results have led to the emergence of a new genre – modern Polish cuisine. This retains the authentic national character, but in a lighter, more interesting version. There has also been a return to rustic cooking. This makes the most of peasant dishes, and tends to be served amidst appropriately bucolic decor. Indeed 'folklore chic' and 'rustic chic', involving the re-creation of 19th-century country inns and manor houses, are the latest design mantras.

Restaurant opening hours are usually very user-friendly, typically from noon 'until the last guest leaves' at around 11pm, midnight, or even later, with meals served throughout the day. Due to the import tax on wine, even *vin ordinaire* can seem expensive. Local vodka and beer are far cheaper. Don't expect cheap restaurants to accept credit cards.

Key to Prices:
Inexpensive: up to 35 zł
Moderate: 35–60 zł
Expensive: 60 zł upwards

Polish

Chłopskie Jadło
ul Św Agnieszki 1
Tel: 421 85 20
ul Jana 3
Tel: 429 5157
ul Grodzka 9
Tel: 429 6187
Chłopskie Jadło ('Peasant's Kitchen') evokes the traditional spirit of Polish-style hospitality in a wonderful replica of a 19th-century country inn. The original, at ul Św Agnieszki 1, has individually decorated rooms featuring furnishings such as an old wooden sledge turned into a table for four. Two rooms resemble a fisherman's hut and the deck of a fishing boat, with murals providing maritime views. Fine country cooking includes the likes of *bigos* (hunter's stew, comprising five different types of meat simmered with mushrooms, cabbage and sauerkraut), and *golonka* (pork knuckle cooked in beer) served with mustard and horseradish. Live folk music revs up the atmosphere. Moderate.

Grand Hotel
ul Sławkowska 5-7
Tel: 421 72 55
In accordance with its name, this is a grand restaurant – classical dishes are served by waiters familiar with old-world standards of courtesy against a background of historic decor. Staff members will help translate and explain a menu that comprises Polish specialities such as sole Walewska, trout and perch dishes, as well as modern Euro-favourites such as seafood cocktails, Parma ham and Chateaubriand. The dining room is a showcase of elegant Secessionism, with a stained-glass dome and ornate galleries at the mezzanine level. Expensive

Piwnica u Szkota
ul Mikołajska 4
Tel: 422 15 70
In keeping with the establishment's name – which means 'The Scotsman's Cellar' – the staff are dressed in kilts. But don't assume that this is a theme restaurant: a trio of large cellars decorated in an antique manner are more samovars and oil lamps than whisky and thistles. The menu does feature Scotch egg and haggis, but these are secondary to

Right: the Grand Hotel's dining room

a wide choice of European and Polish dishes typified by frog's legs in breadcrumbs, *żur* (rye soup) and pork stuffed with prunes. Moderate.

Pod Aniołami
ul Grodzka 35
Tel: 421 39 99
Pod Aniołami ('Under the Angels') is, quite justifiably, one of Kraków's most popular restaurants. It's located in a large cellar decorated with less-is-more 'folklore chic' touches, and featuring open cooking ranges. A lovely patio garden at the rear is perfect for *al fresco* dining. An extensive menu of Polish favourites is complemented by some interesting regional cuisine. The grilled *brinza* (smoked ewe's cheese, a speciality of the Tatra Mountain highlanders) starter is a real highlight. Moderate.

Szabla i Szklanka
ul Poselska 22
Tel: 426 54 40
A visit is recommended to this snug Polish–Hungarian restaurant, adjacent to the Wawel Hotel. The decor is a modern take on Hungarian style, dotted with naive touches and splashes of colour, and the service is knowledgeable. Start with the delectable goose and mushroom pie with plum sauce; followed perhaps by veal chops with pumpkin seeds, garlic sauce and mash, and ginger cake with rose jam and nuts. Moderate/Expensive.

U Pani Staśi
Entrance at Mikołajska 16
This restaurant presents the cheapest way to enjoy good home cooking. The way to approach it is via a passageway to an inner courtyard, where you will probably have to join the queue. The menu posted by the door and the few that circulate inside are in Polish only, but don't expect waitresses to listen patiently if you don't speak the language (or even if you do). The restaurant opens at 12.30pm and closes when the food has all been eaten, usually by late afternoon. *Barszcz* (beetroot soup), buckwheat and *pierogi* (ravioli filled with curd cheese and mashed potatoes or, for dessert, apples) are recommended. It's not a place to linger – tell the cashier on the till what you had and pay up. Inexpensive.

U Babci Maliny
ul Sławkowska 17
Tel: 422 70 66
In keeping with its name (meaning 'At Your Granny Malina's') this eatery serves up dishes typically cooked by a Polish granny. It's all great value. Classic peasant food – fermented rye soup with potatoes and sausage, *grochowka z grzankami* (pea soup with croutons), *placki ziemniaczane* (grated potato pancakes) – is served in generous amounts. Order at the counter and pick up a number, which flashes on a small screen when your meal is ready. Collect the food yourself, and take your finished plates to the hatch. Inexpensive.

Wentzl
Rynek Główny 19
Tel: 429 57 12
Wentzl offers a classic Polish menu extended by Viennese specialities. Given its imposing pavement facade, and the ground-floor café's icing-sugar colour scheme, the 'fine-dining' restaurant in the cellar is something of a surprise. The decor is best described as a meeting of vaulted antiquity with postmodern metalwork sculptures. Expensive.

Wierzynek
Rynek Główny 15
Tel: 424 96 00
The grandee of all Kraków's restaurants, this

Left: friendly service is the norm

establishment occupies two Renaissance houses which were beautifully renovated in the 19th century. Customers can dine in one of several rooms, each individually decorated. The menu is a compilation of Poland's greatest culinary hits: house specialities include boar steak and buckwheat cooked in lard (which tastes far better than it sounds). The 14th-century cellar offers a wide range of fondues and grilled dishes. There is a café for light snacks and traditional favourites such as hot spiced beer and spiced mulled mead and wine. Expensive.

Vegetarian

Salad Bar u Chimera
ul Św Anny 3
Tel: 423 21 78
This salad bar is situated beneath the more formal U Chimera restaurant and comprises several interlinked, high-ceilinged, brick and stone vaulted cellar rooms. The tables are well spaced and the atmosphere pleasant. Everything tastes fresh, and is served in a friendly manner at the counter. Choose from the likes of herring salad, stuffed tomatoes and various quiches. Inexpensive.

French

Cyrano de Bergerac
ul Sławkowska 26
Tel: 411 72 88
Proud winner of the Best Restaurant in Galicia award. This achievement might not sound like a big deal in a region not known for the quality of its dining establishments, but Cyrano de Bergerac would be a contender whatever the locale or standard of competition. The fillet steak is excellent, as are the Polish highlights, such as *pierogi* (similar to ravioli). A superb list of French wines befits the superior wine cellar setting of high ceilings and antique furniture. There is also a delightful courtyard garden for *al fresco* dining during the summer months. Expensive.

Restauracja Szara
Rynek Główny 6
Tel: 421 66 69
French, Italian, European and Polish classics, served in a brasserie-style setting, with vaulted ceilings bearing original art nouveau motifs, and views over the market square.

Italian

Amarone
Pod Różą Hotel
ul Floriańska 14
Tel: 424 33 81
Amarone's large atrium-style dining room blends the trappings of modernity with some carefully placed Etruscan (pre-Roman) details. In particular, look out for the elegant metalwork gallery that accommodates the bar. A few separate dining rooms offer an excellent 'Roman villa'-style eating experience. If you're happy to stick with standard Italian fare, there's a good range of dishes from that country. A great start is being served an amuse-gueule (a mini pre starter that, in Kraków, is a real innovation), followed by a main course of *pappardelle* (ribboned macaroni) with wild mushrooms, and a dessert of almonds in chocolate sauce. An extensive Italian wine list is another bonus. Elegantly dressed tables attract a suitably dressed-up crowd. Expensive.

Cherubino
ul Św Tomasza 17
Tel: 429 40 07
A Tuscan/Polish menu includes delicious favourites from each cuisine: antipasti, minestrone, risotto, pierogi. One dining room contains 18th- and 19th-century carriages and an ornate tiled stove, the other is rustic-chic Tuscan, with a wood-fired oven and a beamed ceiling. Moderate.

Cyklop
ul Mikołajska 16
Tel: 421 66 03
This is a friendly establishment whose simple decor follows the familiar trattoria formula. It enjoys a reputation for serving the best pizza in town, which is cooked in a traditional wood-burning oven. It is deservedly popular, so expect to queue during peak hours. Inexpensive.

Da Pietro
Main Market Square 17
Tel: 422 32 79
A spacious and elegant cellar restaurant with professional, attentive staff and an engaging 'smart-casual' atmosphere, Da Pietro seems

Polish. Highlights include chicken *kneidlach* (dumplings) in dill sauce, stuffed goose necks, and carp with ginger sauce. Moderate.

Ariel
ul Szeroka 18
Tel: 421 79 20
Choose from pavement tables overlooking the street, a sheltered patio courtyard with a goldfish pond, or the conservative, 1970s-style dining room with paintings depicting Jewish life. There's also plenty of choice on the Polish/Jewish menu, with classics such as herring fillets in sour cream, chicken soup and *pierogi* (ravioli) stuffed with curd cheese. A small bookshop in the entrance hall sells guidebooks and souvenirs from Kazimierz. Moderate.

Klezmerhojs
ul Szeroka 6
Tel: 411 12 45
The hotel café has the air of a bourgeois home – oil paintings, vases with roses on each table, and comfortable sofas and armchairs make for a very pleasant scene. The restaurant manages to be more formal and more stylishly bohemian at the same time. Jewish and Polish dishes include excellent *chłodnik* (cold beetroot soup with sour cream and dill) and baked cheesecake. Moderate.

Cafés
Jama Michalika
ul Florianska 45
Tel: 422 15 61
One of the most famous cafés in Poland, with amazing art nouveau interiors and a bohemian history. Great cakes. Inexpensive.

Bankowa
Rynek Główny 47
Tel: 429 56 77
Small, exquisite art nouveau café with al fresco tables overlooking the market square. Inexpensive.

Kawiarnia Noworolska
Sukiennice 1
Rynek Główny
Tel: 422 47 71
Art nouveau café with individually decorated rooms, and al fresco tables within the arcade of the sukiennice. Inexpensive.

to have a large base of regulars who dress up for the occasion. It's a reputation for reliable, enjoyable Italian food, comprising all that country's classic dishes, that keeps people coming back for more. Moderate.

Metropolitan
ul Sławkowska 3
Tel: 421 98 03
Metropolitan is one of the chicest restaurants to have opened in recent years. The architectural blend of assorted styles into a 'modern classic' look complements a fine menu that covers Italian, French and Polish cuisine. And the service is excellent. Moderate.

Villa Decius
al 27 Lipca 17a
Tel: 425 33 90
It's a bit of a trek to reach this eatery from the centre of town, but it's worth the effort to dine on well-prepared Italian, Polish and other European dishes within the palatial Italianate Renaissance Villa Decius. The restored building is a feast in itself. Expensive.

Jewish
Alef
ul Szeroka 17
Kazimierz
Tel: 421 38 70
Antique sofas, candelabra, oil paintings and vaulted ceilings – together with live music every evening from 8pm – create a bohemian, *fin-de-siècle* town-house feel. The menu leans more towards Jewish traditions than

Above: Ariel in Kazimierz serves classical Jewish fare such as herring fillets in sour cream
Right: after years of communist austerity, there are now lots of upscale cafés and bars

Paparazzi
ul Mikołajska 9
Tel: 429 45 97
Modern, Manhattan-style, with great cocktails and Italian dishes. Moderate.

Redolfi
Rynek Główny 38
Tel: 423 05 79
Dating from 1823, the city's oldest café retains an early 19th-century style. Inexpensive.

NIGHTLIFE

Kraków's nightlife, ranging from opera to discos, caters for the bohemian lifestyle associated with university cities everywhere: avant-garde theatre, rowdy drinking sessions and all-night dancing.

The cinemas screen Polish and foreign films, the latter not long after their Western European premieres. Foreign movies are generally screened in their native language with subtitles. Tickets are inexpensive, with most box offices opening an hour (or sometimes 30 minutes) before the performance.

Only a few venues stage theatrical productions in any language other than Polish. Drama covers the spectrum from experimental works to the classics. Sometimes entire seasons are given over to ballet and opera, the latter usually sung in the original language.

The Philharmonic presents an eclectic classical music programme, and Wawel Castle hosts a season of concerts. Jazz is popular – venues in the centre offer trad and progressive jam sessions. Discos and late-night bars (often with music and dance

floors), get very busy in summer and some stay open all night. Entrance is usually cheap.

For information on cultural events, the **Cultural Centre** publishes *Miesiąc w Krakowie (This Month in Kraków)* complete with listings and English-language section. The **Centrum Informacji Kulturalnej** (Cultural Information Centre) can give you the lowdown at ul św Jana 2 (tel: 421 77 87).

Cinema
Kraków Cinema Centre
ul św Jana 6
Tel: 421 41 99
The most popular cinema complex in the city centre, with three deluxe auditoriums and an atmospheric café decorated in a 1930s style and featuring a collection of old radios.

Pod Baranami
Main Market Square 27
Tel: 423 07 68
Cinema housed in a historic palace.

Kijów
al Krasińskiego 34
Tel: 422 30 93
Mikro
ul Lea 5
Tel: 634 28 97
Panasonic IMAX
al Pokoju 44
Tel: 290 90 90
Paradox
ul Krowoderska 8
Tel: 430 00 25 ext 51
Pasaż
Rynek Główny 9
Tel: 422 77 13

Theatre

Stary Teatr im Heleny Modrzejewskiej
ul Jagiellońska 1
Tel: 422 4040.
Kraków's and Poland's oldest theatre has three auditoriums. There's a museum of the history of the theatre and, in the basement, a bar that's very popular with thespians.

Teatr im J Słowackiego
(Juliusz Słowacki Theatre)
pl św Ducha 1
Tel: 422 45 25
Kraków's top theatre stages plays, operas with Polish subtitles, ballet, and fringe events on the *scena miniatura* (miniature stage).

Teatr Bagatella
ul Karmelicka 6
Tel: 422 66 77
Children's productions and adult classics.

Teatr Groteska
ul Skarbowa 2
Tel: 633 37 62
Modern Polish plays, plus a short summer season in the marquee.

Scena Stu
al Krasińskiego 16/18
Tel: 422 27 44
Productions and recitals staged in repertory.

PWST Scena im St. Wyspiańskiego
ul Straszewskiego 22
Tel: 422 15 92
Polish and foreign plays.

Dining with Live Music

Pod Zlotà Pipà
ul Floriańska 30
Tel: 421 94 66
Polish and Viennese dishes served in red-brick cellars. Live music – Russian, gypsy and jazz – starts at 8pm on Fri and Sat.

Cafe Sukiennice
Main Market Square 1/3 (in the Cloth Hall)
Tel: 422 24 68
Attractive modern café with a Euro-Polish menu and live music playing Thur–Sat evenings.

Cabaret

Café Cabaret
ul św Jana 2
Tel: 421 96 37
Regular shows, plus monthly performances by Poland's most renowned satirists.

Jama Michalika
ul Floriańska 45
Tel: 422 15 61
This Secessionist café continues a cabaret tradition that originated in 1905.

Loch Camelot
ul Św Tomasza 17
Tel: 423 06 38
Popular 'rustic chic' café that stages intimate cabaret and recitals.

Pod Baranami
Main Market Square 27
Tel: 421 25 00
One of the country's finest cabaret venue, providing future stars with an apprenticeship.

Pod Wyrwigroszem
ul Św Jana 30
Tel: 431 18 00
Quick-fire satirical cabaret set in attractive cellar location.

Zielone Szkiełko
ul łobozowska 3
Tel: 422 3122
Reputable cabaret housed within an arts club.

Jazz

Harris Piano Jazz Bar
Main Market Square 28
Tel: 421 57 41
Students and professional performers jam together throughout the week.

Kornet
al Krasińskiego 19
Tel: 427 02 44
The resident band play traditional numbers, with guest artists providing regular variety.

U Louisa
Main Market Square 13
Tel: 421 80 92

Internet café with jazz and blues playing at weekends.

U Muniaka
ul Floriańska 3
Tel: 432 12 05
Long-established jazz venue under the auspices of Janusz Muniak, a top performer.

Piwnica Pod Ogródkiem
ul Jagiellonska 6
Tel: 421 6029
Popular venue with a varied repertoire. Good food and a pleasant atmosphere. Open from 1pm until the last customer leaves.

Classical Music
Opera i Operetka
ul Lubicz 48
Tel: 421 16 30
Frequent foreign-language productions of operas and operettas (with Polish surtitles).

Panstwowa Filharmonia im. Karola Szymanowskiego (National Philharmonia)
ul Zwierzyniecka 1
Tel: 422 94 77
Home to Kraków Philharmonic and Choi. Historic and contemporary music.

Polskie Towarzystwo Muzyki Dawnej
ul Westerplatte 10
Tel: 422 0064
Chamber music and, in September, an international festival of ancient music.

Late Night Bars and Clubs
Atmosfera
pl Szczepański 7
Atmospheric cellar bar. Occasional live music.

Black Box
ul Mikołajska 24
Tel: 421 18 63
Cool, funky cellar. In summer there's also an *al fresco* bar under parachute awning.

Free Pub
ul Slawkowska 4
Tel: 802 90 82
This is one of the city's best nightclubs, which explains why it's always crowded. Only closes when the last guest leaves.

Prohibicja
ul Grodzka 51
Tel: 422 86 41
Grungey, double bat cave with smoky 'twilight' zone in which to hang out.

Discos
Kredens
Main Market Square 20
Tel: 429 20 07
Well-appointed cellar venue that's usually swinging. Free admission.

Pod Jaszczurami
Main Market Square 8
Tel: 429 38 37
Discos are held at the weekend, live shows during the week. Hot, frenetic and fun.

Emergency Club
ul Łazarza 9a
Rock- and soul-oriented disco music.

Pasja
ul Szewska 5
Tel: 42 30 483
Glam disco floor. Also pool tables.

Pod Baranami
Main Market Square 27
Tel: 423 07 68
Disco cabaret venue.

Wolności FM
ul Królewska 1
Tel: 423 47 05
Westernised venue. Retro nights play sounds of the '60s and '70s. Disco at weekends.

Above: the Pod Jaszczurami disco features live performances on week nights

CALENDAR OF EVENTS

Kraków enjoys a calendar of diverse artistic and cultural festivals. Catholic festivals are celebrated in the traditional Polish manner.

Easter is one of the most important festival in the Roman Catholic year. On the Thursday prior to Lent, known as 'Fat Thursday,' the tradition is to eat lots of *pączki* (doughnuts filled with rose-petal jam) and *chrusty* (deep-fried pastry fingers dredged in icing sugar). On Palm Sunday, palms are taken to church to be blessed. Holy Week is a solemn period prior to Good Friday, which in turn entails a symbolic fast during which locals typically confine their diet to herring and rye bread.

On Easter Saturday the provisions for a traditional Easter breakfast are taken to church in decorated baskets to be blessed. These comprise hard-boiled eggs, sausage, ham, rye bread, salt and horseradish, plus plenty of cakes, including cheesecake, poppy seed cake and the Easter *babka*, a tall, fluted yeast cake flavoured with chocolate and vanilla.

On Easter Monday locals have a very good reason to get up early – they want to participate in a traditional ritual known as '*śmygus dyngus*'. Until noon everyone has the right to splash people with water. The victim has no rights and is not supposed to retaliate. For centuries groups of young boys have roamed the neighborhood looking for unsuspecting girls on Easter Monday. A gentle sprinkle of cologne water is considered restrained and gentlemanly behaviour, but some insist on drenching strangers with jugs full of cold water.

The **Feast of the Assumption of the Blessed Virgin Mary** is commemorated on 15 August with a special mass at Wawel Cathedral; **All Saints' Day** on 1 November involves processions of locals taking candles and flowers to the graves of relatives.

The most important element of the **Christmas** festivities is *Wigilia*, the traditional dinner held on Christmas Eve, after a symbolic meatless fast during the day (herrings and rye bread). The *Wigilia* meal traditionally comprises 12 dishes, one for each apostle. It is supposed to begin on the appearance of the night's first star, which symbolises the star that guided the Three Kings.

As this is a holy day, the entire meal is meatless – even animal fat is excluded. The Christmas Eve *barszcz* is consequently based on vegetable rather than meat stock. This is followed by fish such as pike, carp and salmon, which in turn is followed by a selection of *pierogi* (similar to ravioli), fruit compote, *makowiec* (poppy seed cake) and lemon tea. Then it's off to church for mid-

Above: Corpus Christi

night mass. On **New Year's Eve** (*Sylwester*), the Main Market Square fills with revellers.

For information on all of these events, contact the Centrum Informacji Kulturalnej (Cultural Information Centre), ul św Jana 2, tel: 421 77 87.

January–February

The **Feast Day of the Three Kings** on the 6th is marked by a special mass. This is the start of carnival, which extends until Shrove Tuesday.

The **International Festival of Sea Shanties** is held in various venues in the last week of February.

March–April

The **Polish and International Festival of Advertising Films and Advertisements** is held in the Kiev Cinema in the first week of March.

From the end of March to the beginning of April, the **Ludwig van Beethoven Easter Festival** is held at venues, such as the Philharmonia and Juliusz Słowacki Theatre.

Days of Organ Music is held throughout Kraków's churches in the last week of April.

May

National Constitution Day on the 3rd is a national holiday marked by the laying of wreaths at the tomb of the unknown soldier.

The **Jazz Festival** is held in the first two weeks.

The **International Biennial of Graphic Art** runs through September on even-numbered years.

International Short Film Festival runs from late May till early June.

The Juliusz Słowacki Theatre hosts the **Kraków Spring Ballet** through July.

June–July

On the eighth day after Corpus Christi, the **Lajkonik Pageant** proceeds through the city to the Main Market Square.

The **Inauguration of the King of the Cockerel Brotherhood** is a folk procession in late June that starts at the Celestat Palace and finishes at the Main Market Square.

Wianki on 20 June is a celebration of the shortest night of the year. On the nearest weekend women float candle-bearing floral wreaths down the Vistula River from the quay by Wawel Castle.

Tyniec Organ recitals are held in the Benedictine Abbey at Tyniec until August.

A **Festival of Jewish Culture** in the Kazimierz district and various venues in the city centre runs from the end of June–early July.

Krakowiak and Góral International Folk Dance and Music Competition is held in the Main Market Square in June.

The Juliusz Słowacki Theatre is the venue for the **Summer Opera and Operetta Festival** from the second week of July.

August–September

The Main Market Square hosts the **International Carnival of Street Theatre**.

The **International Festival of Music** in the last two weeks of the month features symphonies, chamber music and recitals at the Philharmonia, churches and in the courtyards of buildings around the Main Market Square. In the third week of September, the Philharmonia and other venues host the **International Competition of Contemporary Chamber Music**.

November–December

The **Festival of Ancient Music** is enjoyed in the second and third weeks of November in various churches.

A **Competition and Exhibition of Christ-Child's Cribs** is held on 2 December by the Adam Mickiewicz Monument on the Main Market Square. The exhibits are displayed until mid-February at the Krzysztofory Museum.

Churches host a **Christmas Carol Festival**.

Right: folk music and dance

Practical
Information

GETTING THERE

By Air

There are direct flights to Kraków's John Paul II Airport in Balice (tel: 411 19 55) from leading European cities – London, Zurich, Frankfurt, Rome, Paris and Vienna – throughout the year. Seasonal direct flights operate from distant cities such as Toronto. Additionally, numerous European and international routes travel to Warsaw's Okęcie Airport, from which there are regular domestic flights to Balice Airport.

Although Balice is only a small airport, it is modern, comfortable and, situated a mere 15km (10 miles) from Kraków, very convenient. Two municipal bus services connect Balice Airport to Kraków and run every 15–25 minutes; single tickets cost 2.5zł. Line 208 runs to the city centre at Nowy Kleparz, and Line 192 goes to Kraków central rail station and Plac Matejki. Both services take around 40 minutes. A taxi ride from the airport to the centre of Kraków should cost approximately 40 zł.

Airlines with offices in Kraków include:
LOT Polish Airlines, ul Basztowa 15
British Airways, ul św Tomasza 25
Delta Airlines, ul Szpitalna 36
Austrian Airlines, ul Krakowska 41.

By Rail

There are frequent express services to Kraków from various European cities including Berlin, Budapest, Frankfurt, Prague and Vienna. There is also a regular train service from London to Warsaw, with express trains throughout the day from Warsaw to Kraków (the fastest journey time is around 2 hours and 45 minutes, but you need to make a prior reservation for express services). For details of trains from Kraków, tel: 422 22 48 or 94 36.

Train station information desks may not be staffed by English speakers, but the colour-coded timetables are fairly easy to

follow. The yellow timetable is for departures (*odjazdy*); the white one for arrivals (*przyjazdy*). Express trains usually feature the prefix '*ex*', and direct trains are indicated as *pospieszny*. Trains marked '*osobowy*' are slow, sometimes very slow. The main railway station is within easy walking distance of the historic centre, though the traffic system obliges taxis leaving the terminus to take a slightly more circuitous route to the centre. Train tickets can also be purchased from travel agents.

By Road

Coach travel is very cheap in Poland. In Kraków, coaches leave from the bus station at Pl Kolejowy by the train station. Various routes are offered by PKS, the state-owned coach company (for information on coach services from Kraków, tel:624 29 45). More modern, privately owned operators include Polski Express (tel: 630 29 67). The coach trip from Kraków to Warsaw can be a long journey because coaches often stop at a number of cities en route. These include Częstochowa (the site of Poland's holiest shrine, the

Jasna Góra Monastery) and Łódz.

Car rental is available through Hertz desks at Balice Airport and at Hotel Cracovia (al Focha 1, tel: 429 62 62, www.hcrtz.com.pl), and also from Avis (ul Lubicz 23, tel: 629 61 08, www.avis.pl). Be sure to have your driving licence and car-rental papers with you whenever you use the vehicle.

Left: trams provide a cheap and reliable way to get around
Right: bilingual signposts make life easier for foreign visitors

TRAVEL ESSENTIALS

Visas and Passports

Visitors from numerous countries do not require a visa in advance – a visa is stamped on your passport on arrival. Visitors to Poland from the USA, European Union and British Commonwealth countries can stay for up to 90 days without a visa. British passport holders can stay for up to six months without a visa. Passports should be valid for up to six months after the departure date. As a precaution it is best to check any changes in the regulations with the Polish embassy in your country of residence prior to departure. On arrival, the mandatory registration process with the local police is automatically undertaken by your hotel.

Vaccinations

No specific vaccinations are required, but you should be up to date with tetanus, polio and diphtheria immunisations.

Customs

Since Poland joined the EU in 2004, duty-free allowances no longer apply. Dogs and cats may be brought into the country, providing they are accompanied by an official vaccination certificate from a vet, which is less than 12 months old and valid at least three weeks prior to arrival. (This document should be translated into Polish). Antiques and works of art produced in Poland before 1945 can only be exported with the appropriate documentation from the curator at the government customs department, at ul Pod Chorążych 1 (tel: 638 46 00 or 638 40 80).

Climate and When to Visit

Winters are crisp and snowy, with December and January typically cold, damp and foggy. Don't let this put you off: when covered with snow, Kraków looks magnificent, and the surrounding attractions, such as Zakopane, Poland's premier skiing resort, are in full swing. Summers are usually hot and sunny from May to September, though September and October can be very wet.

Clothing

During the winter a warm coat, hat and gloves are required; even during the summer a light raincoat and waterproof shoes are a sensible precaution.

Electricity

Poland uses standard European plugs and adaptors. The current is 220 volts.

Time Differences

Polish time is one hour ahead of Greenwich Mean Time.

GETTING ACQUAINTED

Geography

Centrally located in southern Poland, Kraków is surrounded by various national parks, historic towns and palaces. To the northwest of Kraków is the Krakowsko-Częstochowska Jura mountain range, part of which incorporates the Ojcowski National Park; to the west is the industrial heartland of Upper Silesia. The wide depression of primarily agricultural land known as Kotlina Sandomierska (the Sandomierz Basin) lies to the east, the Tatra Mountains to the south.

Government and Economy

Poland has one of the fastest growing economies of all the former Eastern Bloc countries, and there have been massive changes since the first postwar democratic elections in 1989. The subsequent process of privatisation is ongoing. As a result of the country's solid economic base and future potential, numerous international companies have set up representative or subsidiary offices in Poland.

The Polish Parliament consists of a Lower House (*Sejm*) and an Upper House (Senate), with the Senate and President able to veto recommendations from the *Sejm*. As of 2000, the right-wing Solidarity Electoral Action (AWS) group has a parliamentary majority.

Religion

The vast majority of Poles are Roman Catholics. A Roman Catholic Mass is said in English at 10.30am on Sundays at Kościół św Idziego (on ul Grodzka).

Although far less common, Kraków also has churches and houses of worship for other denominations and faiths. These include

Kościół św Marcina (Church of St Martin) and on ul Onul Grodzka Baptystów (Baptist church) on ul Wyspiańskiego for Protestants, and for Jews, there's Kazimierz's Remuh Synagogue on ul Szeroka.

How Not To Offend

Churches, synagogues and other places of worship should not be visited during Mass or other religious services. For churches that are accessible only during Mass, you should be discreet, and certainly not take photographs. There is always some time immediately after Mass has ended and before the church is closed in which you may look at the sights.

Population

Kraków is Poland's third largest city and has a population of almost 750,000. The vast majority of the population is accounted for by Poles, with tiny ethnic groups including Jews, Germans, Ukranians, Lithuanians, and expatriate communities (generally British, American and German).

MONEY MATTERS

Currency

Poland's currency comprises złoty (paper notes and coins) and groszy (coins): 100 groszy equals 1 złoty. Groszy coins come in denominations of 1, 2, 5, 10, 20 and 50. Smaller denominations of złoty (1, 2 and 5 złoty) are coins; higher denominations (10, 20, 50, 100 and 200 złoty) are in the form of paper notes.

Credit Cards

Internationally established credit cards, including American Express, Visa and Mastercard are accepted by numerous hotels, restaurants and shops. Don't expect smaller establishments to accept credit cards, particularly not for minimal sums.

Cash advances on credit cards can be arranged at a number of banks, including PEKAO, Main Market Square 31. Be sure to bring your passport. There's an American Express counter at the Orbis travel agent, Main Market Square 41. You can also cash travellers cheques here.

Cash Machines

There are Cirrus cash machines, which accept international credit cards, throughout the centre. You'll find one at the PEKAO Bank (Main Market Square 31), at numerous other sites in the square (Nos 21, 23, 41, 47) and at ul Floriańska 6.

Tipping

It is customary to tip restaurant staff, taxi drivers and hotel staff, such as the porter, around 10–15 percent.

Taxes

Retail prices, restaurant and hotel bills include value added tax at 7 percent.

Bureaux de Change

Various banks throughout the city centre exchange foreign currency, although better rates are usually offered by exchange kiosks and counters (marked '*Kantor*'), which are usually conveniently easy to find. These include kiosks at ul Floriańska 40 and ul Sławkowska 4.

Be extremely wary of strangers who offer to change money for you. They will either be attempting to pay you a lower rate or, if their deal sounds particularly attractive, they are probably trying to pass off counterfeit bank notes.

Above: strolling around Sukiennice

GETTING AROUND

Taxis

Although the town centre is essentially pedestrianised, taxis do have access. There are cab ranks around the Main Market Square. Not that it's very practical or even necessary to use taxis to get around the centre. Radio taxis, which can be booked by phone, are generally cheaper than taxis from ranks, though the latter are not very expensive. For longer journeys, negotiate the fare with the driver before departure.

Train

The main railway station, a short walk from the historic centre, is Kraków Główny. You can catch a train from here to Kraków Płaszów, in the Płaszów district, where there are train connections to the Auschwitz-Birkenau concentration camp and also to the Wieliczka salt mine.

Bus and Tram Tickets

Bus and tram tickets are available from newsagent kiosks, or on board from the driver (the latter option adds a surcharge of 0.5 zł per ticket). Daily and weekly passes are also available from municipal transport offices. Tickets must be punched into the ticket machines inside the bus as soon as you board. There are no conductors, but ticket inspectors regularly board buses to check passengers' tickets. Inspectors apply on-the-spot penalties of 96 zł to anyone travelling without a valid ticket.

If you buy a single ticket and are carrying luggage bigger than 20cm x 40cm x 60cm, (8in x 16in x 24in) you'll have to buy an additional ticket (for 2.4 zł) or pay a fine of 72 zł, in addition to the ticket price. You can carry luggage free of charge if you have a day or weekly pass.

A wide range of tickets is available. A single-fare ticket (2.4 zł) is valid for one journey. A one-hour ticket (3 zł) is valid for all journeys within one hour of the ticket being punched. A day pass (10 zł) is valid throughout the day; also available are 48-hour tickets (18 zł), and 72-hour tickets (24 zł), including night services. Bus and tram routes operate from 5am to 11pm, after which the night service takes over. A single journey ticket for night services is 4.8 zł.

If you plan to take a bus trip beyond the city boundaries, a yellow ticket (2.4 zł) for '*linie strefowe*' is valid for single journeys (including any part of the trip within the city). For bus and tram information, tel: 910.

Bus Routes

Bus routes with numbers in the '200' range, such as 201, 202, are suburban and long-distance services operating beyond the city boundaries. Buses numbered in the '500' range are express services that do not stop at every bus stop on the route. Buses numbered in the '600' range operate a night service. A growing number of privately run 'micro-buses' operate various routes around the centre. Tickets, which are a bit more expensive than on public transport, are available from the driver.

Car

Cars should only be parked in guarded car parks (a necessity due to the rise of break-ins and car theft). There are only two car parks in the historic centre, at Plac św Ducha and Plac Szczepański. Neither are very large and

both are very popular. Additional car parks within walking distance of the centre include Plac Kolejowy, by the main railway and bus stations, ul Wielople, ul Zyblikiewicza, ul Karmelicka, ul Straszewskiego, and ul Powiśle by Wawel Castle.

On the River
Boat trips are an ideal way of seeing some of Kraków's historical sights even though the river does not run through the centre of the city. These can be boarded at the pier by Wawel Castle.

HOURS AND HOLIDAYS

Business Hours
Business hours are typically 9am–5pm.

Public Holidays
1 January – New Year's Day
March/April (variable) – Easter Monday
1 May – Labour Day
3 May – Constitution Day
June (variable) – Corpus Christi
15 August – Feast of the Assumption
1 November – All Saints Day
11 November – Independence Day
25 December – Christmas Day
26 December – St Stephen's Day

Market Days
Groceries can be bought every day from the markets at Rynek Kleparski (between ul Basztowa and ul św Filipa) and from stalls around the main bus and railway stations. There are numerous flower stalls in the Main Market Square and also the occasional antique and flea market on a Sunday. In the historic Jewish district of Kazimierz, you can buy groceries Mon–Sat from the market on Plac Nowy, where a flea market is also held on Sunday mornings.

ACCOMMODATION

There are lots of hotels within the historic centre, ranging from 'mansion house' to town house, at a range of prices, all with a distinctly local atmosphere. These hotels do not have extras such as nightclubs, gyms

Left: a horse-drawn carriage awaits
Above: watch out for trams

and swimming pools, but what they don't have by way of facilities, they compensate by their character and location. If you hire a car, don't expect these central hotels to provide parking space (at best a very limited number of spaces may be available).

Larger, more modern hotels, with a range of sporting and leisure facilities, are located reasonably close to the city centre. Either add extra time to your itineraries to reach the centre on foot, or add the extra expense of travelling by taxi.

Most hotels offer a flexible range of accommodation, with single and triple rooms usually available, and the possibility of asking for an extra bed in a double room. Even some of the town-centre hotels have rooms without bathrooms as a budget option. All rooms in expensive and mid-range hotels have direct-dial phones and TV (unless otherwise stated).

Approximate pricing categories, based on a standard double room per night, are as follows:
$ = $40–$75
$$ = $75–$110
$$$ = $110–$150
$$$$ = over $150

Expensive
Hotel Francuski
ul Pijarska 13
Tel: 422 51 22, fax: 422 52 70
www.oribs.pl
Renowned as the city's leading hotel, not least by foreign VIPs. The *fin-de-siècle* style, dating from the hotel's inauguration in 1912, was thoroughly refurbished prior to re-opening in 1991. The restaurant serves good Polish and French cuisine. Ideally located opposite the Czartoryski Museum, adjacent to the Planty Gardens and a few minutes from the Main Market Square. $$$$

practical information

Elektor Hotel
ul Szpitalna 28
Tel: 423 23 17, fax: 423 23 27
www.hotelelektor.com.pl
A range of suites with lounges ideal for business travellers. The restaurant serves traditional Polish food, and there's an attractive wine bar in the cellar. The hotel also administers the adjoining Elektor Aneks. **$$$$**

Grand Hotel
ul Sławkowska 5/7
Tel: 421 72 55, fax: 421 83 60
www.grand.pl
Near the Main Market Square, this traditionally furnished hotel is over 100 years old. Secessionist features include stained-glass panels and 'wedding cake' dining room. **$$$$**

Hotel Copernicus
ul Kanoniczna 16
Tel: 431 10 44, fax: 431 11 40
www.hotel.com.pl
Modern hotel behind a renaissance facade, with a pool and atrium courtyard, close to the Wawel Castle. **$$$$**

Radisson SAS Hotel
ul Straszewskiego
Tel: 618 88 88, fax: 618 88 89
www.radissonsas.com
Modern, deluxe hotel well-placed for the Old Town and the Wawel Castle. **$$$$**

Sheraton Krakow
ul Powiśle 7
Tel: 662 16 60
www.sheraton.com/krakow
Luxury and modernity, with an atrium courtyard garden, in a central location. **$$$$**

Moderate
Hotel Pod Różą
ul Floriańska 14
Tel: 424 33 00, fax: 421 75 13
www.hotel.com.pl
Located by the Main Market Square in one of the centre's premier streets, this historic hotel has some impressive period features, such as the mid-19th century neoclassical entrance portal. Modern additions include the Amarone Italian restaurant, which is one of the city's finest. **$$**

Hotel Polski Pod Białm Orłem
ul Pijarska 17
Tel: 422 11 44, fax: 429 18 10
www.podorlem.com.pl
Comfortable hotel next to the Czartoryski Museum and Florian's Gate, overlooking the original city walls. **$$**

Hotel Polonia
ul Basztowa 25
Tel: 422 12 33, fax: 422 16 21
www.hotel-polonia.com.pl
A recent thorough refurbishment has spruced up this elegant, neoclassical hotel. Situated by a key traffic junction, the hotel is directly opposite the Planty Gardens, a few minutes from the main railway station. Amenities include a beauty parlour and garage. **$$**

Hotel Europejski
ul Lubicz 5
Tel: 423 25 10, fax: 423 25 29
www.he.pl
A few minutes' walk from the Planty Gardens and Juliusz Słowacki Theatre, this period building offers flexible accommodation, including an attractive, 'mansion-block apartment suite' at around the price of a double in a town centre hotel. Cheaper rooms are also available (shower only). There is a stylish bar, a new restaurant and parking. **$$**

Hotel Royal
ul św Gertrudy 26–29
Tel: 421 58 49, fax: 421 58 57
www.royal.com.pl
This handsome Secessionist building, dating back to 1898, has a great location directly opposite Wawel Castle, within the Planty Gardens and just a short walk from Kazimierz. The interiors reflect the Secessionist style. The less expensive 2-star section offers a choice of single, double, triple and even quadruple rooms. **$$/$$$**

Hotel Ester
ul Szeroka 20
Tel: 429 11 88, fax: 429 12 33
www.hotel-ester.krakow.pl
New hotel in the heart of Kazimierz, opposite the Old Synagogue museum, and within walking distance of Wawel Castle. Its small scale (50 guests maximum) lends a personal

touch. A smart, contemporary-style restaurant serves Polish and Jewish cuisine, there's a bar in the cellar and parking spaces. Big reductions can be had in winter. **$$**

Hotel Eden
ul Ciemna 15
Tel: 430 65 65, fax: 430 67 67
www.hoteleden.pl
Fine new hotel in the heart of Kazimierz. With sauna and garden. **$$**

Hotel Pollera
ul Szpitalna 30
Tel: 422 10 44, fax: 422 13 89
www.pollera.com.pl
Opposite the Juliusz Słowacki Theatre and Holy Cross Church, next to a guarded car park. Beyond the classical facade, delightful Seccessionist interiors thrive in the café and restaurant, while details include a floral stained-glass window on the staircase. **$**

Klezmer-Hois
ul Szeroka 6
Tel/fax: 411 12 45
www.klezmer.pl
Located on the principal street of Kazimierz, near the Tempel and Remuh synagogues, this *fin-de-siècle*, town-house hotel has an attractive café and restaurant. **$**

Budget
Hotel Saski
ul Sławkowska 3
Tel: 421 42 22, fax: 421 48 30
www.hotelsaski.com.pl
The hotel closest to the Main Market Square, this attractive 16th-century building features a splendid ornamental elevator. Flexible accommodation, with traditional and modern furniture, offers competitive options such as a double or triple without bathroom. **$**

Hotel Fortuna
ul Czapskich 5
Tel: 411 08 06, fax: 430 1004
www.hotel-fortuna.com.pl
This newly renovated period building with a nicely furnished restaurant, café and bar, is located in a neighbourhood of eclectic late 19th-century architecture. It's within walking distance of the centre. **$**

Right: the Hotel Royal occupies a handsome Secessionist building

Hotel Wit Stwosz
ul Mikołajska
Tel: 429 60 26, fax: 429 61 39
www.wit-stwosz.com.pl
A couple of minutes walk from the Main Market Square, this historic building dating from the 16th century has recently been renovated in a traditional style. An atmospheric cellar restaurant serves Polish food. **$**

Hotel Monopol
ul św Gertrudy 6
Tel: 422 76 66, fax: 269 15 60
www.rthotels.com.pl
Behind its neoclassical facade, this modest, 2-star hotel (refurbishment planned but not yet scheduled) makes an excellent budget option, being situated just across the road from the Planty Gardens. Various categories of rooms, all of which have a phone but no TV, include triples and what must be the least expensive suites in the town centre. **$**

Rycerska
Plac na Groblach 22
Tel: 422 60 82, fax: 422 33 99
Pension in a period building with adjoining restaurant that serves Polish food, located by Wawel Castle. Less expensive rooms (without TV and bathrooms) also available. **$**

Other Accommodation
PTTK Wyspiański
ul Westerplatte 15
Tel: 422 95 00, fax: 422 57 19
www.hotel-wyspianski.pl
Renovated former hostel, with single, double and triple rooms, opposite Planty Gardens. **$**

Hotel Letni
Bydgoska 19
Tel/fax: 637 4433
A small number of rooms (generally without bathrooms) are available throughout the year; a larger number of rooms (with bathrooms) are available in the summer season. This hostel has cheap single, double and triple rooms, as well as dormitory-style accommodation for up to four guests. Other options include single, double or triple rooms with a kitchen. There's an inexpensive eatery on the premises, plus a disco and a billiards table. In a quiet location by a park, but it's a bit of a trek to the centre. **$**

Waweltour
ul Pawia 8
Tel: 422 19 21/422 16 40
This accommodation bureau books rooms in private homes, in the historic centre as well as further afield. For rooms in the peak months of July and August reservations must be made well in advance. Open Mon–Fri 8am–8pm, Sat 8am–2pm.

Camp Sites
Krakowianka
ul Żywiecka Boczna 2
Tel: 268 14 17
Smok
ul Kamedulska 18
Tel: 429 72 66

HEALTH & EMERGENCIES

Hygiene/General Health
It is best to drink bottled rather than tap water. In addition to various bigger-name brands, mineral waters from Polish spas are readily available.

Pharmacies
There are numerous pharmacies (*Apteka*) throughout the city, offering a 24-hour service, including ul Krowoderska 31, and ul

Galla 26. For information on all-night pharmacies, call 661 22 40.

Emergencies
In an emergency, call 999 for an ambulance, 997 for police or 998 for the fire brigade. Alternatively, call directory enquiries 913 and ask for the nearest hospital casualty department.

Medical/Dental Services
It is best to have comprehensive medical insurance, even if your country of residence has a reciprocal agreement with Poland for medical care (for example basic medical care is free for British citizens).

Centrum Medicover (tel: 9677) operates a network of medical centres in Poland's major cities, including Kraków. Medicover has English-speaking staff, a broad range of specialists and an ambulance service. Its programme includes home visits, and it will treat non-members. Medical services are also provided by Falck (tel: 9675) and Scanmed (tel: 412 07 99).

Dentists who speak foreign languages can be booked at the private clinic Dental America, pl Szczepański 3 (tel: 421 89 48), and Royal Medical, ul Zwierzyniecka 29 (tel: 431 1585).

Crime
Although Kraków is generally peaceful, all cities pose a potential threat, so take sensible precautions. Areas to be avoided late at night include the main railway station, the Planty Gardens and ul Westerplatte.

Toilets
Not only is there a serious shortage of public toilets in Kraków but, whether it's a public convenience, or in a café or restaurant, the user invariably has to pay for the privilege. Vigilant attendants demand that you cough up the cash as per posted prices – usually anything up to 1 zł.

COMMUNICATIONS & NEWS

Post Offices
There are two main post offices in the city centre. One is located by the main railway

Left: policemen in conference

and bus stations, at ul Lubicz 4. This is open 24 hours a day all week. The post office at ul Westerplatte 20 (tel: 422 03 22) is open throughout the week 7.30am–8.30pm, Sat 8am–2pm, Sun 9am–2pm. The public telephone boxes are accessible 24 hours per day, all week.

Telephones

Public telephones can be found throughout the city. They will accept tokens ('*żetony*', available from post offices) or cards, but not coins. Only local and national calls can be made from phones accepting tokens.

International calls can be made from phones that accept magnetic cards, which are available from post offices in various denominations – 25, 50 or 100 units. For the national and international operator, and for operator-assisted calls, tel: 900.

When calling other Polish cities the preceding '0' must be included in the city code. For example, to telephone someone in Warsaw, dial 022, followed by the subscriber number.

For calls abroad, dial the international access code, 00, then the country code:

UK – 44
USA and Canada – 1
Germany – 49
France – 33
Spain – 34

If using a US phone credit card, use the following numbers:

AT&T – 0 0800 111 11 11
Sprint – 0 0800 111 21 22
MCI – 0 0800 111 31 15.

Among several internet cafés in the centre is The Internet Café, 23 Main Market Square, offers 24-hour internet access, with various options including multi-login tickets valid between midnight and 6am being the cheapest deal at 0.95 zł per hour. International courier companies include UPS, ul Powstanców 63, tel: 412 3238.

Media

Polish broadsheets include *Dziennik Polski* (*Polish Daily*) and *Gazeta Wyborcza* (*The Electorate's Newspaper*). Glossy celebrity and lifestyle magazines are becoming increasingly popular.

Of the various English-language listings magazines, *Welcome to Kraków* and *What, Where, When Kraków*, are available free from hotel foyers. *Kraków in Your Pocket* (5zł) is available from newsagent kiosks, as are Polish publications with comprehensive English-language sections, such as *Karnet Kraków Cultural Events* (3 zł), and *Miesiąc w Krakowie* (4 zł), which has '*This Month in Kraków*' as a subtitle.

Empik (Main Market Square 5) has a fine selection of European and American newspapers and magazines.

Television

In addition to terrestrial channels, including two state-run stations, and TV Polonia, there are several Polish satellite channels. Most hotels have satellite TV offering English-language stations such as CNN.

Radio Stations

A growing number of radio stations include Radio Kraków on 101.6 EM, and Jazz Radio 101 FM. Radio Plus on 93.7 broadcasts some English-language programmes.

USEFUL INFORMATION

Disabled

For detailed information about facilities and services for the disabled and disadvantaged, contact one of the following organisations: Ogólny Związek Inwalidów (The Polish Association of Invalids) al Daszynskiego 22, tel: 422 8063.

Krajowe Towarzystwo Autyzmu (National Autism Association) ul Bałuckiego 6, tel: 266 1102.

Polski Związek Gluchych (The Polish Association for the Deaf), ul św Jana 18, tel: 422 39 94.

Above: red is still the colour when it comes to postboxes

Polskie Towarzystwo Walki z Kalectwem (Polish Association Campaigning on Behalf of the Disabled), ul Dunajewskiego 5, tel: 422 28 11.

Polski Związek Niewidomych (The Polish Association for the Blind), ul Podbrzeże Berkajosalewicza 2, tel: 422 97 16.

Children

Not surprisingly in a city with such a long and colourful history, and in a country with little extra money to spend on frivolity, Kraków's attractions are definitely geared towards adults rather than children.

Of the children's entertainment that does exist, everything is performed in Polish, so if you are visiting the country with youngsters who don't speak the language, you might have to devise your own distractions.

However, you should find plenty of opportunities for child-friendly fun and games in some of the following places: Kraków's green areas (the Planty Gardens, the Park H Jordana with children's play areas, the botanical gardens), the zoo (open daily all year; ul Kasy Oszczędn M Krakowa 14, Wolski Forest; tel: 422 52 22), at sporting venues and in the pedestrianised centre.

Bookshops

In addition to Empik at Main Market Square 5, the best bets for bookshops featuring English-language sections are:

Ksiągarnia Hetmańska, Main Market Square 17.

The English Book Centre, Plac Matejki 5.

Columbus, ul Grodzka 60.

The bookshop at the Galicia Jewish Museum, ul Dajwór 18.

Massolit Books, ul Felicjanek 4.

LANGUAGE

In addition to Polish, English and German are the most widely spoken languages. Prior to 1989, schoolchildren were obliged to learn Russian, which these days, in keeping with prevailing Polish attitudes towards that country, remains a highly unpopular language.

SPORT

Indoor swimming pools

Korona Sports Club, ul Kalwaryjska 9 Tel: 656 02 50.

Wisła Sports Club, ul Reymonta 22 Tel: 610 15 62.

Park Wodny, ul Dobrega Pasterza 126 Tel: 616 31 90.

Outdoor swimming pools

Krakowianka, ul Bulwarowa 1. Tel: 644 14 21.

Clepardia, ul Mackiewicza 14. Tel: 415 16 74.

Tennis courts

Zwierzyniecki Sports Club and Tennis Centre, ul Na Błoniach 1. Tel: 422 04 15.

Horse riding

The Kraków Horse Riding Club, ul Niezapominajek 1. Tel: 425 25 48.

Decjusz, ul Kasztanowa 1. Tel: 425 24 21.

USEFUL ADDRESSES

Tourist Offices

Tourist information can be obtained from offices at the following addresses:

ul Pawia 8; tel: 422 60 91; open Mon–Fri 8am–4pm and, in the summer season, Sat 9am–1pm.

Małopolska Region Tourist Information Office, Main Market Square 1–3 (within the Cloth Hall); tel: 421 77 06; www.mcit.pl; open Mon–Fri 9am–6pm, Sat 9am–4pm.

For information on cultural events beyond the details published in listings magazines, you should visit the Centrum Informacji Kulturalnej (Cultural Information Centre) at ul św Jana 2; tel: 421 77 87; open Mon–Fri 10am–7pm, Sat 11am–7pm.

You can get information on Jewish-related events from the Jewish Cultural Information Office located at Kazimierz, Centrum Kultury Żydowskiej, ul Meiselsa 17; tel: 430 64 49, fax: 430 64 97; www.judaica.pl; open Mon–Fri 10am–6pm, Sat–Sun 10am–2pm. Tourist information on Kazimierz is also available at ul Józefa 7, tel: 422 04 71, open Mon–Sat 10am–6pm, Sun 10am–4pm.

Polish Tourist Offices
Outside Poland
United Kingdom:
Polish National Tourist Office
Westec House, Westgate, London W5 1WY.
Tel: 08700 675012, fax: 08700 675011.
www.visitpoland.org

USA:
Polish National Tourist Office
275 Madison Avenue, Suite 1711
New York, NY 10016
Tel: 212 338 94 12, fax: 212 338 92 83.
www.polandtour.org

Germany:
Pölnisches Informationszentrum für Touristik
Marbrger Strasse 1, 10789 Berlin.
Tel: (30) 21 00 920, fax: 21 00 9214.
www.polen-info.de

France:
Office National Polonais de Tourisme
49 Avenue de l'Opera
720002 Paris
Tel: 42 44 19 00, fax: 42 97 52 25
www.tourismc.pologne.net

Italy:
Ufficio Turistico Polacco
Via Vittorio Veneto 54 A, 00-187 Roma.
Tel: 482 70 60, fax: 481 75 69.
www.polonia.it

Sightseeing Tours

Other tourist and travel offices include the
following, where sightseeing tours and travel
in Kraków and Poland can be arranged:
Orbis, Main Market Square 41.
Tel: 422 40 35.
www.orbis.krakow.pl
Gromada, Plac Szczepański 8; tel: 422 61 60.
Intercrac, ul Krupnicza 3.
Tel: 422 58 40.
www.intercrac.com.pl
Point, ul Armii Krajowej 11.
Tel: 636 01 51.
Jordan, ul Długa 9.
Tel: 421 21 25.
Jan-Pol, ul Westerplatte 15-16.
Tel: 421 27 26.
Email: btp@janpol.com.pl

Right: Sukiennice

Foreign Consulates in Kraków
General Consulate of the Republic of Austria, ul Krupnicza 42. Tel: 421 97 66.
General Consulte of the French Republic, ul Stolarska 15. Tel: 422 18 64.
Consulate General of the Federal Republic of Germany, ul Stolarska 7. Tel: 421 84 73.
Consulate General of the United States of America, ul Stolarska 9. Tel: 422 12 94.
Honorary Consulate of the United Kingdom, ul św Anny 9. Tel: 421 70 30.

FURTHER READING

Insight Guide to Poland, Apa Publications.
Expanded and updated guide, with comprehensive descriptions of the sights, background features, detailed travel tips, full-colour maps and stunning photography.
Old Polish Legends, by F.C Anstrutter. Enjoyable book describing traditional Polish tales and legends.
Poland's Jewish Heritage, by Joram Kagan. Short history of the Jews in Poland.
Between East and West, by Anne Applebaum. US journalist's account of her travels through Poland.
Kraków: City of Museums, by Jerzy Banach (ed). Focusing on the city's museums.

ACKNOWLEDGEMENTS

Photography by	**Gregory Wrona** *and*
15, 16, 32, 69, 88	***Jerry Dennis***
86	**Kaplan Productions**
87	**János Kalmár**
Front and back covers	**Gregory Wrona**
Cartography	**Berndtson and Berndtson Productions**

© APA Publications GmbH & Co. Verlag KG Singapore Branch, Singapore

The author would like to thank the Polish Tourist Board, LOT Polish Airlines in London and the Europejski Hotel for helping with travel arrangements. He also wishes to thank the churches and synagogues of Kraków, the National Museum and its various branches, Kraków Tourist Information offices, the Kraków Cultural Information Office and the Botanical Gardens

credits

INDEX